The B.A.L.A.N.C.E Book

14 Simple, Soulful Techniques to Remind You of Your Awesomeness

Jennifer Tuma-Young

Copyright © 2017 Jennifer Tuma-Young

All rights reserved.

ISBN: 1979982961
ISBN-13: 978-1979982962

To Grandma Millie, Grandma Mary, and Miss Mary Lou -
the original inspiristas.

THE LEGAL STUFF AND A NOTE
Some Legal Stuff! This book is written as a source of information only. The information contained in this book should by no means be considered a substitute for the advice of a qualified medical professional, who should always be consulted before beginning any new diet, exercise, or other health program and before taking any dietary supplements or other medications.

The author and the publisher assume no responsibility for any adverse effects arising from the use or application of the information contained in this book.

Products, pictures, trademarks, and trademark names are used throughout this book to describe and inform the reader about various proprietary products that are owned by third parties. No endorsement of the information contained in this book is given by the owners of such products and trademarks, and no endorsement is implied by the inclusion of products, pictures, or trademarks in this book.

THE INSIDE SCOOP

Prelude - You Rock   1
Chapter One
Slowing Down in a Drive-Thru World
The 3 Critical Fuel Sources   5
Chapter Two
B is for Brain Dump and Breathe   30
Chapter Three
A is for Assess and Accept   58
Chapter Four
L is for Let Go and Laugh   81
Chapter Five
A is for Add In and Appreciate   94
Chapter Six
N is for Navigate and Notice Nature   128
Chapter Seven
C is for Confront and Connect   154
Chapter Eight
E is for Engage and Experience   182
Acknowledgments   201

INTRODUCTION
You Rock!!

Don't believe everything you think.
-Dr. Wayne Dyer

Years ago, I wanted to begin a new venture. Not with work (although that was part of it), but with my whole life.

And there was this little voice inside my head that kept telling me:

" Just do it. Take the darn leap, and don't look back; just spread your arms out and believe that you will fly. Believe that you will soar. Believe that you are being who you are meant to be. Let your dreams be your wings, and go for it."

But, then, there was this other voice.

The little voice that told me:

"Be practical. Be realistic. Your life is fine as it is now. You don't need to make a change. You've got responsibilities. You've got bills. And no time. You definitely don't have time to change anything, start something new, chase a crazy dream. You are an adult."

She had a point. So I decided to take the little voice, the not-so-positive little voice out dinner. I thought I could win her over with my enthusiasm, my tenacity, my choice in fabulous sushi hot spots.

I thought, " Sure she thinks that now, but wait 'til she hears my plan. She'll believe in me!" We'll have a little chat, me and that little negative voice, and she will come to the other side. I couldn't wait to convince her that I was worth it.

But, after a nice long meal, she still stuck her tongue out at me. She said excitedly:

"This was fun! You're such an understanding friend. I put you down, I squash your dreams, and you take me to dinner!"

This was the only grin I got out of her the whole night.

So, that's when I decided to get the check and drop her off at the nearest bus station. I deleted that little negative voice from my phone, my iPad, my email, my head, and said my goodbyes.

It wasn't easy. She had been a part of my life for so long, but it was time. If I wanted to move forward, I had to break my ties with the little negative voice.

That same night, me and the positive little voice had a cup of tea, and began creating our vision!! And we never looked back.

So Long Status Quo

I wrote the story of "little miss negative" back in 2009. I wrote it to remind myself that listening to the negative voices whether inside my head or in the world around me was like having dinner with someone who laughs at you the entire time.

We just shouldn't entertain the negativity.

I'm not talking about cutting human beings out of our lives because they are a little "Negative Nancy". Not at all. I just believe we shouldn't allow negativity to keep us feeling suffocated, keep our gifts buried, make us keep up with the Jones', or keep our life at status quo when we were meant to live fully, out loud, shining our lights, connecting with one another, and comforted by a peace no human can deliver alone.

I've struggled with this little negative voice throughout my life, which is why I began to explore how to overcome it over 20 years ago . And the one thing I learned is we don't overcome it ever 1000%. But we can find JOY, be in BALANCE, and love ONE ANOTHER, in spite of it. The 14 techniques in this book are a compilation of the work I've done over the past two decades. But, trust me, I'm still learning always, and the one thing I know for sure is that you already have all the answers within you.

Introduction - You Rock!!

You are an Inspirista

I came up with this term one day while speaking with a friend. She mentioned the word fashionista—a person devoted to fashion—and my immediate thought was, "I'd rather be an inspirista!" Then I sat down with my notebook and pen and defined what that meant:

An inspirista is a woman who has a positive attitude, an inner glow, and a contagious energy that makes others want to smile. She takes challenges in stride and doesn't allow a failure to hold her back or a risk to scare her off. An inspirista turns failure into success; her test becomes her testimony.

An inspirista finds and embraces beauty in herself and the world around her. She lives every day to the fullest. She inspires people to live with love, to follow their passions, and she serves the world by using her unique gifts to help others.

What are the B.A.L.A.N.C.E Techniques?

I am a 'words girl', so it's natural for me to make acronyms to easily remember information. When I started working with women, I began to see some common threads with myself and many of my clients. 'Balance' was a topic that came up often. That's where the quest began - I've studied, researched, earned certifications, researched some more, read books, taught classes, and have coached many women over the years. The B.A.L.A.N.C.E Techniques were derived from all of that, and they still evolve all of the time. In short, they are:

<u>Brain Dump and Breathe</u> so you can clear your mind and listen more closely to your heart.

<u>Assess and Accept</u> so you know who you are and what you stand for.

<u>Let Go and Laugh</u> to lovingly release that which no longer serves you or the greater good.

<u>Add-In and Appreciate</u> so you can enrich your life and the lives of others.

<u>Navigate and Notice Nature</u> so you can use your values as your compass and find JOY in the JOurneY.

<u>Confront and Connect</u> to peacefully resolve conflict and overcome obstacles along the way.

<u>Engage and Experience</u> this beautiful gift of life!

*I wish I could **show** you when you were lonely or in darkness the **astonishing light** of your own being... - Hafiz*

Chapter One
Slowing Down in a Drive-Thru World :
The 3 Critical Fuel Sources

We should all do what, in the long run, gives us joy, even if it is only picking grapes or sorting the laundry. ~ E. B. White

I came into this world like a lightning bolt, without a doctor or an epidural. I was ready and not even a snowstorm could stop me. And, it's funny, because that's how I lived my life too, I spent the better part of my younger years in a rush for no reason— I was a bit of a stressaholic. My mother pointed this out to me a few years ago. "Jennie, honey, you can't sit still. You are always busy with something." I realized she had a point, but I was not alone. Most of the women I knew were the same way:

Busy. Strung out. Searching.

Even when I could help the women I worked with find more time, shortly after something else would come up to cause their speed of life to increase. This speed would definitely affect the way they nurtured themselves, and cause ripple effect in all aspects of their lives. If they got a job promotion, the celebration lasted only a minute, because soon they would be e-mailing at all hours of the night, wishing they had a lighter workload, waking up late, and grabbing a to-go bagel from a convenience store. If their kids were the star athletes, pride would soon be wiped away by exhaustion from the three-day little league World Series, not to mention the parties, trophies, and drive-through dinners on the way home from volunteering in the clubhouse.

I realized the answer to really helping people—which I longed to do and was why I got into business in the first place—was encapsulated in what my mother said to me: help them stop searching and find balance.

The first lesson I learned on my quest was to slow down. The frenzied pace of everyday life plays a huge role in hindering us from being in balance. Thanks to nonstop advances in technology, we can print photographs in an instant, send messages with the click of a button, and cash a check without even leaving our computer. The call for convenience has literally taken over our lives. The downside to this crazy-busy lifestyle is that it leaves us tired and stressed.

We're overextended and overworked, juggling a million things as we run from one responsibility to the next. And when physical or emotional hunger strikes, we're likely to appease it with a quick trip to the convenience store, vending machine, or fast-food restaurant. I learned the key to slowing down in a "drive-through" world was to first define what balance meant for me. And I decided "balance" didn't mean juggling dozens of balls and being terrified of dropping them.

Rather, it meant making choices regarding which items on the to-do list deeply mattered, which items I wanted to hold on to, and which I had to choose to lovingly release...for my sanity and strength, because God gave me the greatest gifts - my children. And I needed to choose wisely for them to have a joyful, present mother. Choosing to be in balance means just that—making choices regarding which "balls" we actually want to hold on to, and which ones we choose to put down. You can begin by answering this question, "What do you want?"

I know, it's a tough question. But by answering it, you will begin setting your own priorities, listening to your heart over the chatter of your mind, learning to say no, and practicing self-care (don't worry—you will learn all about how to do these things throughout this book). By creating standards for your own behavior and the behaviors you tolerate from others, you clear junk out of your life. You begin focusing on the things that bring deep joy and releasing the things that don't honor your core values. And, in doing this, you create time and space for healthy habits.

You can also slow down on a daily basis, taking a few moments here and there to mindfully focus on what you're doing—even when it's just a routine action such as drinking coffee or greeting a neighbor.

Chapter One - Slowing Down in a Drive-Thru World

Take Action
Put on the Brakes

Choose to consciously slow down with everything you do: chew your food, savor your morning coffee, enjoy the steam of the shower, make eye contact and connect with every person you see (from the bank teller to your neighbor to your coworkers to your family members). Plan a home-cooked meal and get the whole family involved in preparing it. Speak slowly. Listen intently. Take at least one regular responsibility off of your plate and delegate it to someone else. Create tech-free times in which your phone is shut off and your computer is out of sight. Just by beginning to slow down, you'll see and feel a shift in your spirit. Don't worry, you'll learn many more techniques to help you slow down throughout this book.

The 3 Critical Fuel Sources

One of the workshops I teach is all about fueling and strengthening 3 critical energy sources / muscle sets. There are so many things that can subconsciously fuel us, and in the wheel of life, the fuel we take in often creates the actions we give out.

Simply put, we have a thought, then we do something. I think about my friend, so I give her a call. I feel hungry, so I eat. These are basics, but as we know, thoughts can be far more complex - so complex that we may get stuck in that place of "overthinking". Overthinking creates stress, and stress creates chaos because it goes against our nature. That chaos, even if not expressed verbally, creates an energy that can pervade every aspect of our lives.

For example, how many times have you replayed and rehashed a scenario over and over in your mind? I think we all have done this. Rehashing is often a cue that something is unresolved. But, replaying the scenario in our mind will not provide resolution, only more tension. This tension can seep into other relationships, our wellbeing, our work performance, and so on.

So how can we live in our natural state of being, present and at peace? Being mindful and in the moment is the simplest way to release all tension.

There are 3 critical fuel sources that when filled properly, enable us to live more fully in this moment. Most people are familiar with one - physical fuel, or food. But the other 2 are equally important - I call them heart fuel and mind fuel.

HEART FUEL is what stirs the soul, excites and energizes you from within. When we're filled up in spirit, we are less likely to turn to external sources to fulfill us. We are also less likely to take offense, because we are more connected with humanity, and we free people from the burden of perfection.

MIND FUEL influences our thoughts. Since we are constantly being subliminally fed Mind Fuel through our senses, we must also consciously choose Mind Fuel that aligns with our heart fuel, so that our thoughts support what "fills up" your spirit.

And, of course, PHYSICAL FUEL means properly fueling our bodies helps us have high energy, a good demeanor, happier moods.

If you don't consciously choose fuel for all 3 of these critical fuel sources, you are subconsciously fed fuel (or subconsciously feeding yourself fuel) that may or may not be in line with the person you are born to be. Choosing with intention assures that you are fueling the 3 sources well.

Now, let's learn a bit more about each of these 3 critical fuels...

****

We are indeed much more than what we eat, but what we eat can nevertheless help us to be much more than what we are. - Adelle Davis

Critical Fuel Source #1
The Food-Life Connection

A few years back, my cousin bought a tank of bargain gas at a service station that he'd never been to before. An hour later, his car broke down; the guys at the garage said the gasoline had been watered down. It cost him a thousand dollars to fix the damage. Now he fuels his car with only high-quality gas from trusted stations.

Not taking good care of our possessions can cause costly problems. We know this. Yet with our most valuable possession—our body—we are often subconsciously careless. We fuel it with drive-through junk and vending-machine mystery food containing ingredients we can't even pronounce. Then we hit the wall by mid-afternoon, depleted and empty.

The type of fuel we take in affects everything we do, say, think, and feel. Low-quality food breaks us down, and high-quality food helps us to be the best version of ourselves possible. It's just like fueling up the car's tank: low-quality gas breaks down the engine, but good fuel keeps it running smoothly.

Food is one of the 3 critical fuel sources - a foundational piece to any change we want to make in our lives. And, if we don't want to make a change, it's still a key component to being our most vibrant selves.

Food is fuel not only to energize our bodies, but also to energize our lives! This was something I had a hard time realizing, because I was always so stuck on food just affecting my weight, I forgot all the incredible wonders of food far beyond the scale. But, when I passed out at Menlo Park Mall many years ago, for the first time in my life, I began to recognize that food played a much more significant role than I was giving it credit for. I now call this the "Food-Life Connection", and mine was clearly out-of-balance.

Restoring balance to your food-life connection is not about depriving yourself through dieting. On the contrary, it's about recognizing the amazing power of food and the connection between food and life. By understanding the food-life connection, and by exploring and restoring your own personal food-life connection, you begin to use food in ways that are more physically and emotionally healthful. You can use food as fuel for your body and as fuel for your life in a balanced way that nourishes your body and your soul. You can transform, reset, and re-balance your food-life connection by taking two very important steps: ditching the dieter's mentality and educating yourself.

Just a Note
Since the rest of the book focuses mainly on the other 2 critical fuel sources, we'll spend a bit more time in this section on physical fuel.

A Little Background
As you may have figured by the heading, this section of the book is dedicated to our relationship with food. When we are fueled well, we think clearer. There is an incredible connection between food and life, and understanding that food is

We all have different reasons for having what I call a 'skewed food-life connection'. For me, it was primarily how my skewed connection began because of how I viewed food as only a means to control the scale. Because I have been every size from 4 to 44, I have spent much of my life labeling myself chubby, chunky, thick, heavy, and—my personal favorite—big boned.

I loathe labels now, if I only knew how damaging they would be to myself, then maybe I would have chosen to be kinder.

But you can have a skewed food-life connection and have never had an issue with weight. A skewed food-life connection can create issues with self-esteem, finances, fear, your pace of life, health, communication, relationships, and so forth. Since food is the basic energy source our physical body needs to thrive, the impact it has on us goes WAY beyond the number on the scale. So while this edition of the book isn't focused on weight, food is still an integral component to implementing the 14 techniques for balance, and a balanced food-life connection is a foundational piece to remembering your awesomeness!!

Your Food-Life Connection

As I mentioned, restoring balance to your food-life connection is not about fixating on food choices to the point that it overtakes your world. It's also about consciously making the best choices on your plate and in your life. When your food-life connection is healthy and balanced, you can enjoy your food and have fun eating without expecting it to fill your emotional emptiness.

It's okay to love food! With its amazing natural powers, food can be healing and serve as comfort when you take time to lovingly prepare a dish for yourself or someone else. I am a total foodie—so much so that I married a chef. I say love it in context—as something that provides fuel, energy, delicious taste, and an enjoyable sensory experience that's often shared with family and friends.

By understanding the food-life connection, and by exploring and restoring your own personal food-life connection, you begin to use food in ways that are more physically and emotionally healthful. You can use food as fuel for your body and as fuel for your life in a balanced way that nourishes your body and your soul.

Throughout this book, I'll be asking you to do some written

exercises, jot down your thoughts, and answer some questions. I recommend that you create a B.A.L.A.N.C.E. Journal for these activities and save the worksheets you create for use with the B.A.L.A.N.C.E. Techniques. Whether you use an inexpensive composition notebook, a fancy leather-bound journal, or your laptop computer, writing is a crucial part of your remembering your awesomeness because it gives power and perspective to your thoughts. It also allows you to gather and record feelings, observations, self-discoveries, and answers to questions in a place where you can easily go back and review, reflect upon, and explore them. You will learn a lot about yourself by looking back at the entries in your B.A.L.A.N.C.E. Journal.

Food-Life Reconnection Step 1:
Ditch the Dieter's Mentality

The dieter's mentality is like a giant cinder block that knocks the food-life connection off-kilter. It forces us to put our lives on hold as we start diet after diet, and to believe that our happiness lies in a pair of size 4 jeans rather than coming from within. Ditching that soul-sapping mentality frees you to look at food in a whole new way.

Instead of viewing food as **fuel for life**, dieters see food as the enemy. We use a designation system that labels some foods as good and others as bad. A good food implies that it helps you lose weight; a bad food implies that it causes weight gain. But food does so much more than control the number on the scale. Food is not the enemy. It is our fuel source, our friend, our energizer.

When you are , the dieter's mentality rules your life. You just don't breathe the same— the thought of food creates a visceral reaction to food that completely shifts the way we show up in the world,

In the dieter's mentality, everything comes down to weight. You are either on or off, up or down, dieting or cheating. The dieter's mentality pushes eating food for health and vitality out of the mix. Tunnel vision limits you to eating for the number on the scale. This mentality clogs your brain and clouds you from being conscious of food's intended purpose. It's time to ditch the dieter's mentality in order to embrace your true food-life connection.

Letting go of it is a process, so let's begin with some simple words. I suggest you remove these from your vocabulary:

Start: as in, "I will start again on Monday." Remember, we don't need to start or stop or go on or off anything. We just need to live and live well. Live like the person you want to be. Begin now and never end. We all make healthy choices and unhealthy choices—that's part of life. If you choose something unhealthy, don't decide that you've ruined your eating for the day and will start over tomorrow, next Monday, next month, or next year. Focus on now! Flush away your regret with a few glasses of water and some movement and make the next choice healthier—which leads us to the second dieter's mentality word to ditch . . .

Bad: as in, "I was bad because I ate a cookie." We all do this. We eat, and we feel guilty. It's unnecessary! Following a bowl of ice cream with a huge serving of guilt does you no good. Not only does it take away the pleasure of the ice cream, but it prevents you from building balance into your eating habits and creating an eating strategy that leaves room for ice cream and other foods you love. Guilt drains you and gives you nothing in return.

Instead of feeling guilty when you eat something in excess, do something about it. Drink some water. Get moving. Did you eat a piece of cake? Dance around the room for a half hour. Have a few french fries? Do some squats in the shower or lunges up the stairs. Hot dogs at the ballpark giving you a tummy ache? Water with lemon all day long will make you feel much better. Just make the next moment healthier, and move forward.

In the following chapters, I'll help you learn to let go of the guilty feelings associated with self-care, food, exercise, and other choices that contribute to your well-being. Feel bad if you rob a bank, not if you eat a cookie!

Wait: as in, "I'll wait to buy new clothes." Or "I'll wait to go to the beach." So many of us believe that we can't start enjoying life until we fit in our skinny jeans. This presents itself with phrases such as: I'll wait to go shopping until I lose five more pounds. I'll wait to start dating until I feel less embarrassed about the size of my butt. I'll skip this year's high school reunion and wait to go next year, when I'm back to my high school size. Forget all that waiting. You are complete, beautiful, and magnificently made now.

The single most magnetic quality about any person I've ever met is the heart —the genuine, from-deep-within beauty that you see when someone is authentic to who they are, cares deeply about humanity, and is compassionate, understanding, joyful. Sometimes we wait, but we are not guaranteed tomorrow. You are beautiful, and you have no reason to wait any longer to live as the awesome human being you are, inside and out.

One Last Thing

The dieter's mentality is notorious for making us feel less than when **any aspect** of our life becomes less than the "ideal". Remember, your clothes size, your bank account, your relationship status, none of that nonsense determines your value as a person. I know this isn't easy to accept, especially when you're constantly bombarded with media images of "perfect" women. Even though it's natural to sometimes feel imperfect, you must remember that you are a person of value no matter what. You are beautiful and unique exactly as you are. Your body is nothing to be ashamed of, and it definitely shouldn't stop you from enjoying life.

Once you ditch the dieter's mentality, change your vocabulary, and accept that you deserve to nourish your body, heart, and mind, you can just breathe and fuel all aspects of your life well .

Food-Life Reconnection Step 2:
Educate Yourself

It's kind of funny: even though I was a champion diet book reader, I actually knew very little about how food impacted my body. I knew how it affected the scale, and I would often label foods as good if they helped me lose weight or bad if they contributed to weight gain. The foods varied depending on my diet of the moment. At one point, if I even looked at bread, I felt bad. At another point, eating pasta was good. I was so turned around by what the word healthy actually meant that I believed a seventy-calorie chemical-filled snack was the healthiest option based on calories alone. I often would fill up on foods that were actually not nourishing, but I thought they were healthy because they were labeled low fat or sugar free or diet.

I finally realized I had to educate myself on what it really means to be healthy. I cracked open books and spent hours online learning about balance, happiness, and health. I decided it was important to understand how the body actually functions, so I learned about digestion, metabolism, and nutrition and why it's so important to drink plenty of water. I took classes on wellness and nutrition and started studying food labels, astonished to discover what junk I had been putting into my body for so many years.

So, let's begin with some basics.

Food and Its Function in the Body

If you understand how your body uses various foods, it's easier to make smart decisions about what to eat.

We'll start with protein. Protein is necessary for building and repairing body tissues, muscles, hair, and nails and is often considered your body's primary building block. Protein helps maintain muscle and keeps your metabolism humming. Lack of protein can contribute to lack of energy, bone density, muscle elasticity, and collagen. At normal levels, collagen helps keep skin supple and young looking. You don't necessarily need a lot of protein, but you do need high-quality protein.

Fat is an excess energy storage system as well as an insulator and lubricator. When food is not available, your body can continue functioning by burning fat. There are healthy fats and unhealthy fats. The healthy fats lubricate your skin, hair, nails, and joints. These fats protect your muscles and bones, raise your high-density lipoprotein (HDL) and lower your low-density lipoprotein (LDL) to create healthy cholesterol levels. Eat healthy fats but only in moderation because they are also high in calories. Good sources include: nuts, salmon, halibut, sea bass, tuna, avocado, flax, olive oil, and canola oil.

Unhealthy fats clog your arteries and are bad for your heart. Fats to avoid (or at least limit) are trans fats, partially hydrogenated fats, saturated fat (found in meats and full-fat dairy products), and deep-fried foods. Hydrogenated fats are often hidden in low-fat foods. One of the worst examples of this is low-fat peanut butter. Manufacturers remove healthy peanut oil and replace it with sugar, chemicals, and partially hydrogenated oils.

Carbohydrates provide energy and fiber. Excess carbohydrates that are not used to fuel your body are converted to fat. Fruits, vegetables, and grains are excellent sources of carbohydrates. Fruits provide natural sugar, which is used for energy, and a variety of vitamins and nutrients that nourish your body. The fiber in fruits helps stabilize your blood sugar levels and promote healthy digestion. Fruits also have antioxidants that fight disease.

Grains provide fiber to cleanse the body. They also provide a long-

Chapter One - Slowing Down in a Drive-Thru World

lasting source of energy, or fuel. Whole, natural grains are better than processed grains. When a grain is refined or processed, it loses fiber and nutrients. Robbed of nutritional value, processed grains provide empty calories that raise blood sugar and turn to fat if not immediately burned. Whole grains are rich in fiber, which helps cleanse your body of toxins. Good sources of grains include: slow-cook (not instant) oat- meal, whole-grain cereals, couscous, semolina, whole-grain dense breads, brown rice, Wasa crackers, and wheat germ. Instant rice, oatmeal, and other grains cook faster, but that's because they are processed.

Because grains are an energy source, remember that the amount of energy you need and when you need it is important. We generally don't need a bowl of oats before we go to sleep because sleep doesn't require energy, right? When we start the day in the morning, it's a different story. Here's a simple rule: unutilized carbohydrates are converted to stored energy, which must be utilized or else is stays on the body.

Vegetables provide fiber, antioxidants, and hydration to the body. They are filled with antioxidants and nutrients for your cells. Low in calories and sugar, they are "free" foods that you can fill up on. It's hard to overdose on veggies, especially the green, leafy kind. It's good to eat them raw, but they're great cooked too. After you begin eating them, your body will crave them more and more. Trust me.

I used to hate vegetables (chomping on celery and carrots alone didn't appeal to me at all). But as I began to learn about vegetables' life-changing, energy- boosting, balance benefits, I sought out new and fun ways to prepare them. I even shredded cauliflower (it had the look and texture of rice) based on a recipe someone shared. It changed my perception of veggies, and before I knew it, I was addicted! Now, my body craves veggies—they are my go-to snack of choice! Once you learn all the benefits of eating vegetables presented in this book, I'm sure you'll learn to love them too.

Food Confessions, Guilt, and the Weight of It All

I had a meeting with a new client a little while back. So, we sat down, and instantly she dumped out all of her food confessions {this happens a lot with new clients by the way, all the time!}. As if I was going to send her to food jail for craving a candy bar every day at noon, or send her to the cleaners for constantly snacking on crackers. Her head was down, as she shamefully shared all of the truths about her eating habits.

She didn't know me at the time, she just signed up for the session because a friend referred her to me. She didn't realize I wasn't going to judge her or try to fix her or make her think she was "less than" because of the size tag in her jeans - no, that wasn't me, that was her putting it all on herself, so I just gave her the space to release it. For some reason one little number can carry so much weight.

Trust me, I get it. My goal was to lift her up so she could see herself in all of her awesomeness, and then share some basic facts about her food choices so she could be gentler with herself, understand herself, and make informed decisions about the foods she was eating.

I mean, there was a perfectly logical and scientific reason why she would constantly snack on crackers. Most crackers are processed carbohydrates, and eating just processed carbs creates a physiological reaction in the body that causes us to crave more of them. They are a relatively low (and not to mention empty) calorie food - we can eat a stack and still not feel full, but so high on the Glycemic Index that the body breaks them down quickly, meaning they release glucose rapidly in the bloodstream creating an insulin response.

The Glycemic Index is also impacted by the Glycemic Load, which basically means if you eat 1 cracker, may not be a big deal on the body, but a stack of crackers increases the load, thereby having a greater impact. It can lead to numerous health issues such as diabetes and may be the reason for my client's lack of energy and feelings of frustration.

We function best and our body performs best when our blood sugar is kept steady.

So, feeling moody? Lethargic? Tired? Hungry? Not your best self? As for my client, this was exactly it - BINGO! She immediately stopped beating herself up with guilt, understood her body better, and began to make a list of snack ideas that would serve her body and life well!

The thing is, food is incredible and is critical fuel for the way we show up and light up in the world - choosing fuels when we're educated and informed makes decision making so much easier. My client said she had heard crackers weren't the "best snack", but since she "didn't buy into the low carb thing", she brushed it off. It's not about a low carb diet or any diet for that matter, it's about honoring the gift of our bodies and being energized to live life fully, to reach our full potential as human beings {which goes so beyond a number on the scale}!

Here are a couple of questions to consider if you are feeling guilt over food ever, trapped on the dieting wheel of frustration, or just know that you are not feeling your best:

1. Are you eating only for the scale?

If no, I am doing a happy dance with you, now move to question 2.

If yes, identify 3 of your core values, your "anchors". Realize that eating for the scale is basically saying you value the number on the scale more than any of your core values, and I KNOW that that's not true!! Focus flipped? Good! Now on to the next question smile emoticon:)

2. Do you understand the affects beyond the scale that your food choices have on your internal body, your organs, and your life?
If no, educate yourself as much as possible on this. Begin simply by asking yourself with every food choice you make, what are the components {or ingredients if it is packaged or pre-made} in this meal/snack? How do these components affect my body?

If yes, and you still are making choices that don't fill you up and fuel you up healthfully, sometimes re-education is helpful to refresh our hearts and minds and re-inspire decision making. Sometimes it's something in another area of our life that needs a little love. There have been so many beautiful, amazing, inspiring women who have come to me over the years feeling "less than". Once we identify our core being, there's a weight that's lifted and we can cut the strings that we are attaching to our worth.

The Benefits of H2O

Drinking water is probably one of the best things you can do for your health. It has a huge, huge impact. One of the very first things I recommend as you set out to balance your life and your food intake is to drink water flavored with fresh lemon. This simple, positive action benefits your body in two ways.

First, if you are dehydrated—as many women are—drinking water with lemon helps you nurture your body by recognizing, respecting, and fulfilling one of its most basic needs. Every organ, tissue, and cell in your body needs water to survive and thrive. You will actually begin to feel more energized, vibrant, and alive as you rehydrate yourself.

Second, drinking water with lemon flushes toxins from your body by helping your kidneys, circulatory system, and sweat glands effectively get rid of unneeded chemicals, waste, and by-products. You will feel less bloated, experience less retention, and all-around feel a little lighter just by drinking H2O.

Not only is it necessary to hydrate the body (which is roughly two-thirds water) and flush out toxins, it is vital to:

- Carry nutrients to our cells
- Absorb nutrients better
- Lubricate the joints
- Get rid of bloat (yes, if you need water you retain water)
- Keep body temperature regulated
- Rev up the metabolism

If you don't get enough water, it's not a matter of just being thirsty. It wreaks havoc on your body and leaves you feeling just plain lousy. If you want to live with energy and passion, you must stay hydrated. Some of the side effects of dehydration include:

- Decrease in energy levels and fatigue
- Migraine (enough said)
- Major digestion issues, which leave toxins in the body
- Retained water that can lead to kidney problems

So, go pour a glass and then keep on drinking! I know there are many prepackaged fancy water alternatives, but they're not necessary. Sixty-four to seventy-two ounces of clear water with fresh lemon every day will give you the maximum benefit.

Don't worry! You can jazz that plain water up yourself simply by adding some citrus (squeeze in some fresh lime, grapefruit, even orange) and mint. Or you can add drops of pure pomegranate or cranberry juice and a mint leaf. If you need a little sweetness, add a pinch of stevia.

Chapter One - Slowing Down in a Drive-Thru World

How much water should you drink? That depends on how much of a water drinker you already are. If you usually never drink water, you can't suddenly start gulping down half a gallon a day. Gradually add it into your day. Choose water with lemon instead of soda, sugary juices, or iced tea. Keep a bottle of water with lemon in your workspace and your car, and drink frequently. If you're not drinking water at all, begin with at least thirty-two ounces a day and go up from there. If you're already drinking some, increase it to sixty-four to seventy-two ounces a day.

****

Every thought we think is creating our future.
- Louise Hay

Critical Fuel Source #2
Mind Fuel and Being Present

You know how you feel when you are sick with a head cold? Tired, run down, dull, and not very productive. The same is true when you have a crowded mind filled with too much mental clutter. You feel tired, run down, and not very productive, not to mention harried, stressed, and inconsistent.

When your mind is crowded, it's stuffed with thoughts and worries about to-do lists, money, time, family, friends, the past, the future, and a million other things. The one thing that you're not thinking about is the present moment.

When you focus on now, rather than the past, the future, and all the things you've got to get done, you open up space to be clear, passionate, inspired, and nurturing. It wasn't until I started practicing presence that I was able to truly listen to God's wisdom, and even still I am human and sometimes the practice goes right out the window! When that happens, I hear squat! But, just like God's grace, being present isn't a one-time thing. It's moment by moment, and it's up to us to make the choice whether to plug into the present moment or not.

There is infinite power in the present moment, but if we are too crowded mentally to appreciate that, we lose out on all that power. We miss beauty. We miss life. We miss opportunity. We miss connecting.

Being fully present in the moment is one of the best and most balancing things you can do for yourself and others. When you are present, you can consciously and intentionally take in fuel for your mind that honors your awesomeness.

Take Action
Stop and Focus

To practice being mindful of the present, begin by focusing on what is immediately in front of you. Say it's a Starbucks coffee cup. Study it closely.

Look only at the cup—don't let yourself think about anything except the shape, texture, colors, and presence of the cup. Spend several moments blocking out everything else and noticing only the cup. Do this a few times to get the hang of it. Then, start trying it out on things that are a bit more important than a coffee cup—the sound of your child's laugh, the color of the sky on a gorgeous winter day, or the taste of a fabulous piece of chocolate melting on your tongue. Listen fully when speaking to others, pay attention. Be present while driving in the car, focusing on the drive and not on your mile-long to-do list. Keep practicing these mindfulness moments and eventually you'll start to feel more present without trying.

Become Aware When Your Mind Isn't There
Awareness is a first key to making a change. While practicing presence and being present can be overwhelming, I often suggest simply becoming aware when your mind isn't there with you in the moment. Then, use a visualization technique to bring you back to center. I have a couple of visualization techniques I like to use myself:

1. The Three Lightbulbs: Think of three lightbulbs. One is in a box in the cabinet, one is in the garbage recently burned out, and one is in the light fixture burning bright. The lightbulb in the cabinet has the promise of energy, the hope of light, but no actual power because it's not plugged in to a present-moment energy source. The lightbulb in the garbage has no power—its power is in the past, gone. The lightbulb in the fixture holds all the energy and power. When you become aware that you are not in the moment, visualize twisting in a lightbulb and watching a bright light appear when it's fully plugged in. That bright light is you, back to center, in this moment, where you have the

Chapter One - Slowing Down in a Drive-Thru World

power to connect, to be, to live fully as the magnificently made human being you were born to be.

2. **Driving in the Car:** Picture yourself driving a car. Imagine you are staring only in the rearview mirror.

   What will happen?

   You'll crash into the car in front of you. Next, imagine focusing on three traffic lights ahead, way down the road. What will happen? You will miss the traffic light that you are approaching and possibly run a red light. Now, imagine driving a car and focusing on the road in front of you, using present-moment energy to push the gas pedal or pump on the break. Now you're in the present moment, rather than looking back at the past or forward into the future.

3. **A Snap Back in the Moment:** This visualization is very simple and is intended to pop you back into the moment. Snap your fingers. Hear the sound and remember it. Do it over and over so it is crisp, loud, and clear in your mind. When you become aware that you are not in the moment, snap yourself back to center.

Being present is a topic that often stirs a lot of questions. It sounds "good in theory", but how can one actually "be present"? I remember asking this once to a very "Zen" teacher in a class I was taking , and his response was that he meditated for 2 hours in the morning and 2 hours in the evening. WHAT?! I laughed as I told him he must not be from Jersey! The people I work with barely have two minutes, let alone two hours!!

But, I learned something important from him, it's not the amount of time but the commitment ~ being present is a daily, ongoing practice, even if you begin by practicing 2 minutes in the morning and 2 minutes in the evening...the commitment to the practice is work {and I understand because I have to work at it} but consider the alternative...

We miss moments when we are not present. Sometimes we miss the beauty of a bird flying past us, the miraculous moment when a flower first blooms, or even the sound of our children's laughter; other times we miss the vulnerable cry for help of another human being lying in the grass or sitting next to us in the office or even at our own dinner table. We need each other for the joys and the pains, but we can only be there for each other if we are fully present in this amazing gift of life.

To continue being mindful, you'll have to begin to free up space in your mind. We'll discuss this in greater detail in chapter 2, but for now, if your mind is racing with thoughts, worries, and concerns, use your B.A.L.A.N.C.E. Journal to clear some of the clutter from your mind. What's swirling around in your head? What are you thinking about? Worrying about? What's sitting on your to-do list?

Write it all down in whatever way feels best—there is no wrong way to do this. You can journal in prose, jot down bullet points, cut out pictures and create a cluttered-mind collage, or create a spreadsheet. The idea is to get your concerns out of your head and onto paper, leaving the space you need in your mind to be creative and insightful and live a passion- ate, inspirational, healthy life.

Critical Fuel Source #3: Heart Fuel
You Have Purpose, Even If You Don't Know What It Is

To know even one life has breathed easier because you have lived. This is to have succeeded. ~ Ralph Waldo Emerson

I shared earlier in the chapter how labels weighed me down. I believe once we are free from the labels, our unique talents emerge even more fully ~ we can just be who we were born to be. Sometimes, though, we don't even know who that is...as many young girls do, in my freshmen year of college, I went through some stuff with self-esteem. By my sophomore year, I was totally lost. I didn't think I was lost at the time of course, but looking back now I know my decisions were being made in an effort to find myself, although I didn't even know what I was looking for. I had a teacher, though, who knowing much of what I was going through, asked me to audition for the school play. I had done theater in high school, but never had a leading role, so I could hardly believe when I saw my name on the sheet.

The play was called Lucia Mad, and I was assigned the role of Lucia. Dr. McGhee believed in me, and he said to my parents the last night of the show, "Jennifer connected with the audience. She drew them into Lucia's story. She didn't think she could pull off the show, but I knew she could."

His words were short but powerful. They stuck in my heart. I didn't feel worthy at all, but he saw a person who connected with people. He also saw me struggling. But he used my personal struggle in a way that lifted me up rather than pulled me down. Because of the nature of the role, {Lucia was struggling in her own ways, too}, Dr. McGhee knew I could share Lucia's journey on stage, even when I thought there was no way in the world I could.

Dr. McGhee was a scholar, a writer, a philosopher. Sometimes I would overhear him talking about his aspirations, doing other work, publishing a book, or moving on to use his talents in other capacities. I was so glad he didn't make that choice before I left the school. I believe he was exactly where he was supposed to be at that time, divinely appointed to lift me up when I really needed it. I will never forget him.

The thing is, I believe we are all divinely appointed things, even if we have no clue about it. Our life, even just a moment of it, can so greatly impact another human being. Even just a few kind words can literally change and shift the course of a person's entire life.

Poof. Just like that. God amazes me with how He uses all of us. And, we don't need to be perfect. Sometimes he uses our imperfections to soothe another human being so they don't feel alone. We connect deeper with each other when we realize our vulnerabilities together. Sometimes, he uses people to show us something or teach us a lesson, to help us stretch or grow. What seems like a dire situation, may actually have much deeper meaning. We are on the surface of it, looking at the junk and thinking, "What is going on?!" or "Why me?!" But, below the surface, there it is, the young, lost girl who couldn't have made it through the year without you.

Think about it - we are assigned jobs, or put in situations like traffic jams or long lines at the food store, and He is up there making all things work together for our good. Unaware, we may be beeping the horn at the car in front of us, and He is saving our lives or someone else's. We may be miserable at work, hating our job, but in the break room we provide a listening ear or open heart for a co-worker going through a tough time, and that is our appointment. That is our purpose. We don't need to search and struggle and find a purpose, knowing we are a magnificently made human being is enough to know we have one.

Now, the tough part is to just let go of the search and appreciate where we are planted, and who we are planted there with. And, what if the hand we are dealt is just plain awful - dealing with loss, illness? Even tougher, realizing that there can be joy in our pain. And there are some things that happen that we simply cannot comprehend.

I guess if we leave it up to our human ambition, it may be easy to continue striving and searching, steamrolling through life as if it were an obstacle course to be conquered rather than a wondrous journey that includes it all - from joy to pain and everything in between. Feeling those emotions makes us alive, and the sheer power of our humanity can be a bit scary or maybe what's beyond is what frightens us. It may be easier to just cut anything that doesn't immediately make us happy out. Clearly not a good solution because before you know it, you can snip it all away down to nothing.

On the flip side, we can also easily slide into stagnant thinking and allow ourselves to be repressed, held down, and dumped on and dragged around by the other people's stuff and our own self-limiting beliefs. It's a delicate balance - when or how do we appreciate our divine appointments and know when we are to be moved into the next?

I know the importance of being in tune, listening within, self-discovery, knowing your anchors, and using your anchors both to center yourself and as a compass to guide and direct your steps ~ I go into this in great detail in my book and classes. To me, since my anchor is my faith, the only real answer is love and service. And to that end, there are more questions...Am I looking at this person or situation through the lens of love, understanding, and compassion? Where I don't understand, can I find comfort in His word or even from another human being appointed to me? How can my life imperfections help or comfort another person? Am I serving humanity in some way?

Mother Teresa once said, "We can all do small things with great love." Sometimes when we do small things with great love, God entrusts us with more. When He gives us more, and we mess up, He appoints us less. It is not anger, but a lesson. We often learn from the assignment, and then He gives us more again. And, He promises to never leave us or forsake us. By knowing He is ultimately the provider and appointer, it takes the worry and burden from us searching, trying to figure out the "what" and "how". The only thing we have to do is show up and light up, and rest easy knowing we are each exactly where we should be.

Chapter One - Slowing Down in a Drive-Thru World

The two most important days of your life are the day you were born, and the day you find out why. - Mark Twain

So how does knowing this fuel our hearts? When we operate from a place of purpose, our body is integral, the way we nurture it is a choice - we can choose behaviors that exemplify love and nurturing, such as:

- Stopping self-criticisms (i.e., asking, "Does my butt look big in this?") and criticisms of others (i.e. being judgmental)
- Practicing self-care, such as movement, exercise, eating well, resting, and being in tune with my body
- Living with passion and energy by using my gifts, helping others, serving, and relying on faith as an anchor
- Creating a space that represents who I am from the inside out: free from clutter, awash in colors I love, filled with visual reminders and inspirations, and decorated with meaningful items
- Practicing love, forgiveness, and understanding of others so I could open up to being gentle toward myself. Life really is a mirror.

Lack of knowing our worth can hurt us dramatically. Often we don't take care of ourselves because we simply don't love ourselves enough. This comes up not only with my friends and in the world, but also all the time in the classes I teach.

When we don't love ourselves, we think nothing of beating ourselves up and taking on guilt and shame. We hurt our bodies with yo-yo diets and extreme exercise regimens because we think we deserve to be starved and deprived. When we love ourselves, we nurture our souls and nourish our bodies. We love exactly who we are in this moment, choose foods carefully, keep our bodies in motion, and surround ourselves with people who support us.

Here are some other ways to know your value:

Reach for your full potential. As women, we are sometimes conditioned to limit ourselves. Not because we are lazy or incapable— we do incredible things all the time, from working and raising children to managing schedules and providing an ear or lending a hand. But it's easy to fall into a rut. If this is true for you, pick a goal and begin to push yourself to achieve it. Take action beyond a daily to-do list of mundane activities and add in something soul stirring and challenging that you can commit to doing.

Let your voice be heard. It's easy to shrink into silence in the corner of a room. When you have unexpressed feelings inside of you, you begin to fall into unhealthy patterns as a means to deal with them. Women who lack self-love often feel that no one cares what they have to say, so they just stop talking and may begin self-destructive habits instead as a means to feel like they are silencing their own voice. I have done this many times in the past. Communication can be difficult, but it's necessary that your voice be heard.

Knowing your worth and nurturing yourself breed confidence, and once you're confident, you can do anything. This sets a good foundation for you to take care of all the other people and responsibilities in your life.

Take Action.
Nurturing Your Worth Strategies
There are so many ways to nurture yourself. Pick one of these suggestions, or choose one of your own, and start nurturing!

- Go for a walk with your best friend.
- Share your thoughtful and honest feelings about something.
- In your B.A.L.A.N.C.E. Journal, write a list of ten personality traits that are uniquely YOU.
- Massage your temples with essential oils.
- Push yourself out of your comfort zone.
- Treat yourself to a bowl of fresh raspberries—and forget about what they cost.
- Make an appointment with your primary care doctor for a full physical exam.
- Play your favorite music as loud as you like.

Strengthening the 3 Critical Fuel Sets

Now that you learned a bit about the 3 critical fuel sets, I want you to also think of them as muscles that need to be strengthened. Again, most people are aware about exercising the body. Just like you fuel your body for energy and you exercise your body to strengthen it, you must fuel your heart and mind, and then strengthen the internal muscle by taking action. For example, fueling your mind with positive thoughts (i.e. reading quotes, listening to books on attitude, surrounding yourself with positive people) is great, but you must strengthen your mind with actions that are also positive - speaking kind words, practicing patience, living with compassion, showing gratitude. And, for example, you can fuel your heart reading the Bible, but you strengthen it by living the Gospel - reaching out and helping others, serving people, giving your talent and your time, etc.

Take Action
Fuel & Strengthen Your Heart and Mind as Well as Your Body

Choose heart and mind-set fuel that will keep your thoughts aligned with your core values. What fuels our minds and hearts is equally (if not more) important to what we fuel our bodies with. And if we don't choose our fuel sources wisely, we can easily lose our focus. Mind-set fuel includes everything you read, listen to, and watch—the things that feed your brain messages. Let go of the mind-set fuel that brings you down.

In your B.A.L.A.N.C.E Journal, begin identifying ways you can fuel & strengthen your heart and mind. List things you currently are doing that support this as well. Think about your 5 senses, as each of these impacts the way we are fueled!

Moving from Myth to Reality

There are so many balance myths floating around. When we buy into them, we block our light from shining.

Once you define and debunk your own balance myths, you can make more centered choices that will move you closer to balance and give you a feeling of power and joy.

Here are some of the most common balance myths:

Myth: I have to attain perfection in order to be balanced.
Reality: Balance is not about having the perfect life, and the more you strive for that, the less fulfilled you will feel. There will always be gaps, and that's okay. Move with the positive, identify what you'd like to create, visualize fun ways to fill the gaps, and have at it! And if you find yourself faced with an imperfection beyond your control, embrace it, and learn from it. Remember, there is so much beauty in that which is imperfect.

Myth: My life would be better if only . . .
Reality: Sure, it's normal to think about the if-onlys in life. If only you had more money. . . . If only you could work less. . . . If only you had time to exercise more. . . . The list goes on and on. Are you weighed down by a bunch of if-only thoughts? I call this the If-Only Syndrome, and I've found that it's a huge energy drainer. Instead of dreaming about if-only scenarios, focus on the joy that surrounds you now. Gratitude for "what is" will naturally make you feel more in balance. We all have challenges in our lives, so keep moving forward, and if you have no clue what to do, be still and listen. Stillness is an action.

Myth: The grass is greener for everyone else.
Reality: Comparison is the thief of joy. Everyone has problems, worries, tragedies, and disappointments—even the people who seem balanced and happy, without a care in the world. They may simply have learned how to put difficulty in perspective and to find joy from within. If the grass looks greener, remember, it takes work to keep that grass green too. Look at the land beneath your feet and lovingly tend it well.

Myth: It's selfish to care for myself.
Reality: Self-care is not selfish; it's necessary. Think about airlines—they always say if you have a child on board with you, in an emergency you must put on your oxygen mask first or else you won't be able to take care of the child. You take care of so many people— your family, partner, coworkers, bosses, neighbors. Human nature drives women to take care of others, but the most effective way to do that is to take care of ourselves too.

Myth: I have to have it all.
Reality: Being in balance requires you to accept that you must define what the term having it all means to you. You may have to let some things go if they are minute in the scheme of your life. Many women strive to succeed at everything. You'll never be happy if you try to succeed at everything because it's impossible. Be clear with yourself about what success really means to you.

I also think success is a mind-set, and begins with recognizing we are successful every day with even the smallest of achievements. For example, some days I feel successful because I made a beautiful scrambled egg for lulu or because I put the dishes away while they were still warm from the dishwasher. This is success for some of us, and we should recognize even the smallest of achievements. Accepting the small successes in our lives allows us to feel more balanced and joyful. If we feel like we can't do anything right, we continually spin our wheels but go nowhere.

Myth: I cannot, and should not, fail at anything.
Reality: I've had clients tell me they feel stuck in a rut and completely out of balance, but fear keeps them at status quo. Truthfully, most successful people aren't lucky; many have failed time and time again. But they've held strong to their vision and their faith, and they accept the inevitability of failure. Fear of failure can be debilitating because it blocks you from taking inspired risks. The setbacks, failures, mistakes, rejections—whatever you want to call them—are just amazing opportunities for growth, learning, or rerouting ourselves and our mission.

Summing up

In this chapter, we've discussed the importance of the 3 critical fuel sources. We went into detail about reestablishing a balanced food-life connection. By doing this, you will see an improvement in energy, a new perspective on food as fuel for life, and remembering your awesomeness. The activities I suggested included the following:
- Create a B.A.L.A.N.C.E. Journal.
- Drink at least thirty-two ounces of water with lemon daily.
- Reconnect with food for its intended purpose: to fuel and nourish your body.
- Fuel your mind and become more aware and present.
- Fuel your heart by knowing your worth.

In chapter 2, I'll show you how to clear your mind of the junk that interferes with your life in balance and how to create a revived life vision.

Chapter Two
B is for Brain Dump and Breathe

An awake heart is like a sky that pours light.
- Hafiz

You're about to learn the first of the B.A.L.A.N.C.E Techniques.. It's time to begin redefining your meaning of a life in balance.

Before we begin, here's something to keep in mind. The B.A.L.A.N.C.E. Techniques can be used in a linear (step-by-step) way, independent in and of themselves, or in any combination that works for you. For the purposes of this book, and to give a sense of structure to begin your journey, however, we will build from one technique to the next.

B.A.L.A.N.C.E Technique #1
Brain Dump: Clear your mind so you can listen to your heart.

I've been a journal keeper since kindergarten, a natural-born brain dumper. I grab a pen and paper whenever my mind feels heavy, and I use my words in ink to release the weight on my brain. I learn a lot about myself through my writing—it is a healing, cathartic process of self-discovery.

I think brain dumping is fairly intuitive: most of us know to at least write a to-do list when we have a lot going on. But I find that brain dumping solely for ourselves happens less and less as our responsibilities increase. Whether we've taken on an intense career or are raising a family or a combination of both, when we are busy, we simply don't prioritize brain dumping for ourselves.

Over the years, I've seen the benefits that brain dumping has had for my clients. First releasing, then reflecting, followed by

Chapter Two - B is for Brain Dump and Breathe

some specific questioning. Brain dumping is an integral part to finding balance and being in balance, because the more you carry in your mind, the heavier you feel physically and emotionally. By dumping out the thoughts that weigh you down, you create time and space for the present moment. The more you release, the clearer you become.

Brain dumping is a fantastic tool that allows you to pour out onto paper the worries, dreams, fears, hopes, regrets, and expectations that are swirling around in your brain. Once you've got them out of your head and onto paper, you can examine them and decide which ones to hold on to, which ones to reframe, and which ones to let go of. It can be a very freeing experience.

Also, brain dumping opens you up to believing in yourself. Somewhere tucked beneath layers of worn experiences, walls of limiting beliefs, years of juggling and balancing and nurturing others, somewhere inside is the real you, the woman you were born to be. She holds the memory of a victory, the lesson from an experience, the call of your purpose. You know that woman well. You just have to extract her memory from all that is clouding your view of her and bring her to the forefront. Remembering and recalling helps you bring her back to life.

Women are amazing. We handle so many things (brilliantly, I might add) on a regular basis. I've seen women overcome debilitating diseases, manage tangles of family finances, raise incredible children, turn passions into careers, and use their skills to help others — yet so many of us fail to see that for ourselves.

But that's about to change. You and I will work together to rediscover the woman you were born to be, awaken you to your awesomeness, and fully recognize your unique talents, gifts, and strengths. God wants to use those gifts to serve the world. Even if one human being is impacted by us fully "plugging in" to our purpose, then it is worth it. The ripple effect we have is incredible.

Brain dumping is a life tool, a technique you can use now and throughout your life to help you clear out all the junk that's clogging your brain in order to make space to live in the present moment, to believe in yourself, to finally hear what's in your heart, to listen to God's direction, and to refresh your perspective. It's a little like taking all the furniture out of a room before you paint and redecorate. Doing a total brain dump will make you feel lighter than you've felt in a very long time.

Let the Brain Dumping Begin

When I meet with women for the first time, they usually ask where we begin. I tell them to start wherever they want and simply tell me what's on their mind.

After a few seconds of awkward silence, the floodgates open and the brain dumping begins. They pour out everything that's going on in their world, in no particular order, but always in a way that eventually connects stories, feelings, and events from different periods of their lives like a crisscross puzzle.

I'd like you to do the same thing, and I've got a few tools that will help you get going.

First, we'll do a free-form brain dump just to get stuff out of your head and onto the page. Next, we'll do a center your focus exercise to shine a light on your strengths, abilities, and past successes to discover your strongest self. Finally, I'll help you create your revived life vision. Using a series of questions, you'll root out the true priorities and core values in every circle of your life— physically, emotionally, socially, and spiritually.

> *Come to me, all you who are weary and burdened, and I will give you rest. - Matthew 11:28*

The Free-Form Brain Dump

The free-form brain dump is all about releasing. It's a process in which you pour out whatever is weighing heavy on your mind— whatever is creating stress, challenges, and the obstacles you're facing in your life. The free-form brain dump process allows you to begin clearing your mind.

For me, I think of this clearing as a way of handing our burdens over to God, and He gives us peace from deep within. In some ways, that alone is enough.

That alone, changes the way we "show up" in the world.

That alone can be the difference between you smiling at a stranger or swirling with a million things in your mind that you miss the other human being entirely. Your smile could be just the moment the stranger needed to feel hopeful.

Chapter Two - B is for Brain Dump and Breathe

That alone can be the difference between you hearing what your daughter is telling you about that's happening in school or just nodding along blankly. Your full attention could be just what she needs to feel valued, loved.

That alone can be the difference between you making peace with an old friend, chatting with a neighbor, encouraging a family member. God wants us to connect with one another. We don't want to miss that opportunity because our mind is too full to be in the moment, nothing is worth it.

Doing a free-form brain dump is simple: grab your B.A.L.A.N.C.E. Journal and start writing. Include lots of details—dump everything out of your head and onto the page.

Where should you begin? Anywhere. Just start writing down what's on your mind. Write in any way that feels comfortable—lists, paragraphs, notes, a letter to yourself, diagrams, even drawings. Whatever works for you—there is no best way to do this—and there's no wrong way either.

There are only two rules in brain dumping:

1. Don't make judgments about yourself afterward.

2. Don't try to fix anything now. Free-form brain dumping is simply about releasing.

If a blank page scares you, here are some starter questions and thoughts to consider:

- What do you hope to learn from this book?
- What is gnawing at your heart?
- What keeps you up at night?
- What is your biggest challenge?
- What is your biggest hope?
- What dreams do you have? What are your gifts?
- How will remembering your awesomeness affect your life?
- What are your fears about change? What excites you about it?
- What do you want?

As you write, allow yourself to be authentic and honest—no one else has to see what you're writing.

Don't even think about what you're writing, and don't worry about spelling, grammar, handwriting, or mentioning what you think you should feel rather than what you truly feel. Just release your feelings and let them flow.

Your goal right now is simply to get everything out and not to evaluate it or draw conclusions—yet. Don't be surprised if you make some pretty powerful discoveries right off the bat. If you experience an aha moment, allow it to happen. But more importantly, don't worry if it doesn't occur. Focus on freeing yourself to release the weight in your mind.

When you are finished brain dumping, take a break. Go for a walk, make a cup of tea, have a meal, or even set your journal aside overnight. During your break, your subconscious mind will start processing what you wrote. You may even start to subconsciously reframe some of your thoughts.

When you're ready, come back and read what you wrote. As you read, try to see connections, discoveries, common threads, and aha moments. What surprises you? What stands out? What troubles you? What elicits a deep emotional response? What observations and conclusions can you draw from what you wrote?

Grab a highlighter and color anything that shows a facet of yourself that stands out. You may want to go over it several times or even read it out loud so you can listen to your thoughts in spoken form. If you want to explore anything more fully, go back and brain dump some more.

When it comes to brain dumping, there are 4 "R's" I like to follow. This technique should assist you to reach your goals in a positive, healthy way:

1. Release It: Grab your journal, and release whatever goals are in your mind. Don't edit them, write them exactly as you are thinking them.

2. Reflect on It: Take a short break - go for a walk, make dinner, just take some time away from what you wrote. After a short break, read it back, and reflect on it. Is there anything you wrote that makes you feel "bad" or "heavy"? Are any of your goals actually "insulting" your current state of life or "putting you down"?

Chapter Two - B is for Brain Dump and Breathe

For example, once a client released that she wanted to "get rid of the Pillsbury Dough Boy rolls on her back." Another client said, "I hate my job. But I'm stuck. I'm old and what do I really know how to do? Maybe I need to go back to school, but I don't have the time or money."

I get it, we all have done this - we beat ourselves up, we talk ourselves down, we dim our lights. Here's the thing - you are amazing! You do incredible things all of the time! And, it's inspiring to have goals, dreams, visions, hopes, so let's set the lens on what we really want, deep within our core. I assure you, your heart would never compare your back to a dough boy or call you old or limit you to a place of discontent. You are magnificently made.

3. Refocus Your Lens: The lens in which we view the world changes our entire experience of it. A shift in thinking opens up the space for the miracle to occur! Powerful. Refocus your lens on what you want, what your heart wants to see. In every moment, there is wonder because all of life is a lesson. For example, if when we look up at the birds in the sky we focus on the one time the bird pooped on our head, we'll feel 'ugh', but if we focus on the beauty of the birds flying above us in the moment, the "ugh" diminishes and grace emerges - it's all we can see. Refocus your lens of life and your goals on what you want, what gives you strength, what illuminates your power.

4. Reframe the Goal: With a new lens and a deep understanding of what you actually want, reframing is natural and easy. In the example of the "doughboy back", my client admitted that seeing those words made her feel awful, and it had been a goal of hers for so long, she realized the awful feeling about herself must have been within her for years. What she really wanted, she said, was a "strong, healthy back". Reframing the goal in this way, she immediately sat up straighter, taller, a light came to her eyes, and she had something solid to work towards. Her confidence came from within. I also experienced this shift myself on several occasions, with all types of goals, and the physical, visible changes from the internal shift in thinking, are not only noticeable but transformative.

How can you reframe your goal to give you something to work towards that allows you to show up and light up in this moment?

Many women who brain dump make some kind of self-discovery—

and sometimes it can be surprising. Realizations lead us to making conscious choices - more often than not, we are operating from the subconscious.

The other beautiful thing about brain dumping is it allows you to see your thoughts in black and white. Then you can choose to reframe your thinking, which allows you to begin to retrain your brain to look at things in a more positive way. Reframing opens you up so you begin to think (and choose) possibilities over limitations, opportunities over challenges, and you begin to focus on that which you can control as opposed to focusing on what you cannot. It also gives God the space to do His work, and us the heart to hear His direction.

Reframing can be a very important, powerful tool. Whenever I brain dump, I notice my fears come out. For my clients it's the same. It's a good time to take our fears and turn them into exciting possibilities.

> *Fear is static that prevents me from hearing myself.*
> *—Samuel Butler*

I know it's hard to just let go of fears, but by focusing on faith and hope instead of fear and despair, we open the door to all good things. Remember, in the space where there is faith, fear cannot stand.

Being fearful is just another way we try to control our lives. It's like our hair—if it's curly, we work hard to make it straight, but one drop of humidity or rain makes it curly again. Life can be filled with so much more joy if we can cut our worry even just in half. So relinquish your fear and let go of all that negative energy. For me, I often get tangled in the worry web, so the only way I see out it is to offer up my concerns to God. Hand them over. The joy we feel when we are weightless is a catalyst for more happiness to be welcomed into our lives and the lives of others.

The key for me is to fix my thoughts on all that is good. Then give thanks for it all. I once read that "worry is a misuse of the imagination." It's true! Worry is created by the same part of the brain that creates hopes, that imagines the possibilities, that is inventive, creative, and bold.

Sometimes worry comes from a place of frustration and exhaustion. When we really want something, we tend to allow it to overtake our whole being, and focus too hard on it. This means we get caught up in trying to figure out how to make it happen. We wait anxiously and anticipate results quickly, and if they don't happen, we get discouraged. If we work too much like a bull, we'll surely ram into stuff. All of this creates stress and negativity, and the response is echoed back to us with more stress and negativity.

Instead, detach from the how. Instead of trying to "make it happen" as the popular quote goes, hold space for it to happen, welcome it, allow it, and take one step at a time. The operative word is not if, it's when. Be still and listen. Sometimes our human ambition isn't in alignment with our purpose. The steps will unfold perfectly, as they should. Bumps become lessons, not blocks.

Take a little time to recognize the weight of your mind. What are you fearful of? Worrying about? Acknowledge it, and then do a visual exercise to wave good-bye to your fears and worries. Put them on a boat, sail them out to sea, watch them float away and disintegrate in your mind's eye.

Brain Dumping as a Technique for Life

Brain dumping is a skill you can come back to throughout your life. You can use it whenever you're feeling stressed, overwhelmed, anxious, or out of balance. It's also a wonderful tool to use when you're facing an important decision or feel like you've hit some kind of crossroad in your life.

The answers to so many of your problems and concerns lie within you. Brain dumping is a simple way to find those answers by clearing out the clutter in your mind and giving you time and peace to tune in to your innate wisdom and to listen to your heart.

Writing is a very effective way to brain dump, but if being alone with a pen and paper scares you or isn't quite your cup of tea, finding a confidant to brain dump with can also be useful. Just be sure it's someone who can understand that brain dumping is just about clearing and releasing, not about debating or seeking judgment or advice.

If you're lucky enough to have an insightful, trustworthy confidant, ask her to help you by posing questions to assist you in self-discovery and reflecting back what you say. Hearing your thoughts spoken back to you is empowering and often leads to aha moments that clarify your thinking and inspire you to change.

If none of your friends or family seems right for this important task, consider scheduling a brain-dump session with a counselor, mentor, or coach.

And, don't forget, God is your perfect confidant. Sometimes just going in my car, driving to a quiet, private area, and releasing it all to Him is the best way for me to brain dump. No pen, no paper, just my presence with Him.

We spend so little time living in the present moment. So often we are somewhere else—replaying something that happened moments ago, dwelling on past mistakes, worrying about the future, going over scenarios of what could/should/might be, or making comparisons with those around us. When all these not-now thoughts bubble in our minds, there is no room for now—the present moment.

Brain dumping is just one way to help you focus your energy on what's directly in front of you. Throughout this book we'll talk about other ways to peel away emotional clutter and live mindfully in the present moment. Learning to quiet the unconscious chatter in your mind allows you to listen better, think more clearly, experience life more fully, connect more effectively, make smarter choices, and enjoy the moments more. When you focus on the present moment, your senses are heightened and you feel more plugged in to life.

Foods That Help Clear Your Mind and Sharpen Your Memory

During the brain-dump process, it's helpful to eat foods that can help clear your mind and sharpen your memory. Yes, you read it right— certain foods can actually help with clarity and focus. For example, foods that are high in vitamin C, vitamin E, and selenium actually con- tribute to mental clarity. Vitamin B helps brain neurotransmitters re- duce cognitive decline, thus improving focus and memory; vitamin B2 (riboflavin) boosts energy and metabolism. Iron enhances brain activity. The following vitamins promote clarity and memory:

- Vitamin C: kiwi, peppers, oranges, tomatoes, papaya, mango, zucchini
- Vitamin E: whole grains, nuts, tomatoes, spinach, broccoli, fish, onions

- Calcium: low-fat dairy products, sesame seeds, tofu, white beans, bok choy
- B vitamins: turkey, tuna, whole grains, lentils, beans
- Selenium: Brazil nuts, tuna, shellfish, cashews, eggs, lentils, sunflower seeds
- Iron: beef, chicken, almonds, and quinoa (pronounced keen-wah, a rice-like food with a rich, nutty taste that is often considered a grain but is actually a seed

By making simple enhancements to our daily food intake, we can choose to enrich our current diets with foods that promote energy, clarity, and overall better brain function! For example, a mango salsa is a tasty addition to any salad, sandwich, or even an omelet.

Clear your mind even more by keeping chopped spinach, onions, and tomatoes on hand to create a topping for chicken, enjoy as a side salad, or add to a wrap. Squeeze some lime juice on edamame for a light and refreshing snack. Sprinkle sesame seeds onto your pasta or in a salad. Add beans to your brownie mix, make quinoa with pine nuts as a quick and tasty side dish.

Ricotta and scrambled eggs make for a simple, healthy, delicious brain dump brunch.

Fluffy, Light Ricotta and Scrambled Eggs with Zucchini Hash Browns

Jazz up scrambled eggs and pack them with the clarity-boosting nutrients mentioned above. It takes less than fifteen minutes to prepare and is filled with flavor, textures, and lots of health benefits.
Serves 1.

What You'll Need
2 eggs
¼ cup part-skim ricotta cheese sea salt
Freshly ground pepper
1 tomato, chopped (optional) 1 zucchini, shredded
¼ onion, chopped olive oil spray

Let's Do This
Mix together the eggs, ricotta, salt, and pepper. For a little extra pizzazz, I like to add a chopped tomato, but you can include whatever veggies you like. Cook them as you would your favorite scrambled eggs.

To make the zucchini hash browns, combine the zucchini and onion and cook in a hot skillet sprayed with olive oil until browned. Flip and brown the other side. You can drain the liquid and form them into patties if you'd like, or just keep them loose.

Center Your Focus

Don't ask what the world needs. Ask what makes you come alive, and go do it. Because what the world needs is people who have come alive. —Howard Thurman

When I was in eighth grade, I was chosen as one of four speakers to give the eighth-grade commencement speech. I was at the podium in my cap and gown describing what it was like to feel like you don't fit in. I told the crowd about my first day of kindergarten. My mother had dressed me in a green plaid kilt with knee-high socks and a cardigan sweater. I was the tallest kid in the class. So tall, I didn't even fit in the desk.

"There I stood, Jolly Green Jennifer," I detailed my experience to an auditorium filled with proud parents, aunts, and uncles. I spoke about the power of kindness, that we shouldn't judge each other because of our differences and flaws, and then I even talked about believing in our dreams.

After I finished, the crowd applauded. Many people came up to me to share their own stories of not fitting in. Others shared dreams they had for the future. I was only thirteen, but I felt on top of the world speaking and sharing a bit of myself that day!

Recalling it now, it feels like yesterday, but for a long while, I forgot about that little girl. I didn't remember that I inspired people, that I had a voice, that I had something to share. Instead, I hid in the corner of a room under a mane of hair practically covering my face.

I made a friend, though, who really liked and accepted me exactly as I was. She didn't see the unworthy girl I saw when I looked in the mirror. She saw the real me, the me who had dreams, loved to help others, and liked to share silly stories. In talking with her, I opened up about myself. She asked me questions about my childhood, happy memories, and fun times, and the eighth-grade graduation speech came up in conversation. The memory of

Chapter Two - B is for Brain Dump and Breathe

that day, the feeling I got from writing and sharing and inspiring, suddenly came back to me and allowed me to believe in myself again.

Brain dumping serves several purposes. We've discussed the importance of releasing what's on your mind to make space for present-moment energy. Now we will move from brain dumping to release to brain dumping to believe.

In order to do this, I'll guide you through the process of defining your core values. Next I'll show you the importance of learning from your own positive life experiences and rekindling your power of creativity and imagination. Then I'll help you create a revived life vision.

But first you have to work on believing in your awesomeness. This belief is like a muscle—you have to work it to keep it strong. It's so much easier to believe in yourself when you are in touch with who you really are, when you are aware of your strengths, gifts, and talents, but more importantly, when you are actually using them regularly to serve others.

In this part of the chapter, we are going to adjust your focus to shine a light on your core values and your individual strengths—what you can do, what you can control. We'll elicit self-discovery through brain dumping about positive past experiences.

When I meet with women, I expect greatness from them— I know that they will do whatever it is they set out to do. I expect that they will succeed. There's no doubt in my mind. If it's in their hearts to do something, create something, achieve something, I know they can and they will.

I know you have the power to do the same thing. I wouldn't be writing this book if I didn't believe every single one of us is infinite in our power. I expect greatness from you. I have no doubt in my mind that you are a complete, whole, capable, incredibly strong and talented human being who can and will live a life of meaning, purpose, and extraordinary value to the world.

I want you to expect greatness from yourself too. You can bring to life whatever you commit to, anything that is in your heart.

Zen Quickie ~ Knowing Your Worth and Defining Your Values

Each of us has a core value system. Our values are the internal compass that guide us through life and anchor us in turbulent times. All the choices you make express your values. Knowing, honoring, and living by your core values makes a huge difference in our overall life experience and sense of purpose.

Overstuffed schedules and stress can cause an (unintentional) lack of focus on what really matters. This lack of focus can disconnect us from our core values. Without an internal compass, we begin attaching our self-worth to things or circumstances, and then we are motivated by those rather than our true values. I was speaking with a dear friend recently, and we were talking about this very subject. Too many of us attach our value to things outside ourselves rather than honoring our inherent worth as humans.

I have two children, lulu and the little Man. They are precious, with imaginations that run wild. When they were little, we would play, we hop around the house like frogs, and we would imagine a café in our backyard where we would hold socials for all our imaginary friends. Now, they use those same imaginations to create artwork, to write, to come up with solutions, to invent, to sing their favorite songs (or even write their own), to have a dance party in our living room, to giggle with their friends on the bus. They are my angels. I could never look at my children and attach their worth to anything.

Why is it so difficult to look in the mirror and do the same thing for ourselves?

We are all worthy. No strings attached. You are worthy.

I know this a hard concept to grasp, because we constantly attach strings to our worth. It is very common in society to attach a person's "worth" to something - an experience, a situation, an outcome. Of course, when we say the words, it sounds ludicrous. But, I distinctly remember (unknowingly) doing this, and I often hear from clients (also many completely unaware) that are attaching their worth to people or things:

* the number on the scale

* the amount of money in the bank account

* the number of clients on the roster

* the way a person looks at them- whether a smile or scowl

...if we allow it, all of these "things" can affect our worth, which in turn affects everything else. Whether a mom is so wrapped up in her children that every last ounce of her worth is tied only to them, or a woman who is so career driven that she never sees family and holidays pass her by, or the juggling working mom who ties her worth to perfection so much that when a ball drops she runs for medicinal help or chocolate...self-worth can be a tangled mess when we attach strings to it.

Here are some questions to consider:

What happens when my children grow up?

Who am I if I lose my job?

What if my business fails?

What if I am not the size I was twenty years ago?

Am I not worthy?

Of course you are! Our essence, who we are each born to be, is not attached to any "thing". No matter what situation life or experience throws at us, no matter what test we are given, we still are worthy. Even when we don't feel like it, even when we want to crawl in a cave and hibernate, we are each whole, complete, capable, resourceful, talented people. But often, that picture gets muddled in the wake left behind by life's experiences.

Let Experience Fuel and Teach

Experiences can be beyond our control. It's hard to separate ourselves from the experience and not somewhat attach our worth to it. But we must. Experience can be used to fuel a fire for the greater good, to teach yourself something, or to teach others. Of course, we each can have moments of feeling down in the dumps. Let the moments last as long as they may, but don't allow the experience to define you or your worth.

Remember, some of most of the amazing movements in the world were born out of strife, terrible experiences, that came full circle and were a catalyst for change- often unplanned, but there is a contagious energy from passion and authenticity born out of a lesson learned from a life experience.

Be Who You Were Born to Be, Do Not Focus on an "Outcome"

When we focus on "outcomes", it affects our worth-

* getting a promotion or not

* opening a business or not

* garnering approval from family or not

* getting recognition or not

* a boyfriend loving us flawed and all or not

* and the list goes on ...

All of the outcomes of these scenarios can easily affect how one feels. Thinking about the "outcomes" first, also affects the path we take. For example, in my 20's I would sometimes think, "If I wear this outfit, then tonight I will probably meet someone." Little did I know my future husband would fall in love with me while I was wearing baggy old sweats and my hair in a knot on top of my head.

I hear from people all of the time who choose a path solely because he/she thinks it will garner the desired outcome. To which I now respond, "what is that outcome for you really about?" Because I've learned, it is never about the outcome. We must delve deeper than that, and do that which makes our soul stir, that which helps others, that which uses our unique gifts to serve the world...and then the "outcomes" do not matter.

Realizing Our Gifts Without Strings Attached

Each of us has unique gifts, that, even when no one is around, even when we are bare, with nothing, we have gifts that need no outcome, no accompaniment. The ironic thing is, many people chase the desired outcome, and along the way, stop using their gifts. And then the outcome never comes. When we simply use our gifts, people flow into our lives, doors open, experiences happen that are

Chapter Two - B is for Brain Dump and Breathe

even bigger than we could have imagined.

Learning by Letting Go of Every "Thing"

I learned I was worthy without strings attached by letting go of almost every "thing". After some financial issues years ago, we sold our home, turned in our vehicle, auctioned off our wedding china, many of the "things" that typically define a person- we shed.

I remember crying, sobbing one day while my baby Lu napped. I prayed to God for an answer, and He told me to write. Writing is something I've done practically since birth. And, for some reason, I didn't even feel worthy of picking up my pen at that time.

Grabbing whatever scrap piece of paper I could find, I started jotting down my thoughts. In that moment, I realized God was telling me it would be alright, to carry on, to continue the work I was doing. We must use our gifts to serve the world. And, a whole new chapter emerged, a peace came over me, that no thing or outcome could ever deliver. It was like the intense love I feel when I hold my children, kiss my husband, see a baby giggle, have a heart to heart with my mom, spend time with my dad, or witness a person truly smiling- that peace stayed with me and I let His love guide me back...I remembered that faith was my anchor- that I am worthy (no strings attached) because I am a child of God.

Every single person, regardless of circumstance, past history, race, color, religion, every single one of us is worthy. Find your anchor in faith, and today, free yourself from the strings that you are attaching to your worth. Choose to look everyone you pass in the eye, listen, share, connect. Be joyful. Laugh. Play. Release fear, ignite your spirit, use your gifts, your talents to help others regardless of any "outcome", and your light will shine bright.

> *"Our deepest fear is not that we are inadequate. Our deepest fear is that we are powerful beyond measure. It is our light, not our darkness that most frightens us. We ask ourselves, 'Who am I to be brilliant, gorgeous, talented, fabulous?' Actually, who are you not to be? You are a child of God. Your playing small does not serve the world. There is nothing enlightened about shrinking so that other people won't feel insecure around you. We are all meant to shine, as children do. We were born to make manifest the glory of God that is within us. It's not just in some of us; it's in everyone. And as we let our own light shine, we unconsciously give other people permission to do the same. As we are liberated from our own fear, our presence automatically liberates others." ~ Marianne Williamson*

What's Your Operating System?

When you operate without honoring your core values, you lose direction; then you look to others for the magic solution when you really have all the answers you need within yourself. To find them, you have to be still, reconnect, and listen.

By reconnecting with your core values, you discover your best self, the magnificent woman you were born to be. You put your values in motion, consciously make an effort to express your values, set goals with your values in mind, and reignite your spark for life.

When you are fully connected to your core values, you find it much easier to let go of behaviors that don't serve you. You create a life free of attachments (to outcomes, possessions, or people) and addictions. You release fear, ignite your spirit, and use your gifts and talents to serve the world. You set value-based standards of behaviors for yourself and others.

Take Action
Identify Your Core Values

Using the list below (and adding any of your own), pick four to six of your most important core values. Be authentic—choose not what you think you should value, but what is in your soul. A value is not something you should be guilted into—it is who you are.

You may hold a number of the values listed below. Remember, too, that our priorities change as we travel through different seasons of our lives. But by honing in on the four to six that resonate most with you in this moment, you will begin to give yourself, your life, and your well-being direction and meaning.

After you've identified your core values, write them down in your B.A.L.A.N.C.E. Journal because we will refer back to them later in the book.

Abundance, achievement, acknowledgment, altruism, appreciation, authenticity, autonomy, beauty, belonging, bravery, camaraderie, candor, certainty, choice, collaboration, comfort, community, compassion, contribution, creativity, decorum, directness, discovery, dreaming, drive, education, excellence, exploring, faith, fame, family, fascination, flexibility, flow, fluency, freedom, friendship, generosity, grace, growth, guidance, happiness, harmony, health, holiness, honesty, hopefulness, humor, imagination, independence, industry, joy, justice, keenness, kindness, leadership, learning, liberation, loyalty, maturity, modesty, nerve, optimism, order, passion, philanthropy, playfulness, precision, privacy, respect, security, self-expression, service, solitude, speed, spirituality, thankfulness, tolerance, tradition, trust, understanding, usefulness, warmth, wisdom, youth, zeal

For a more extensive values list, check out my blog, Inspired Girl (http://inspiredgirl.net/list-of-values). You can also work with a coach trained in values programs.

Learn from Your Experiences

It's kind of funny, but for some people it's easier to recall and retell bad experiences than good ones. A friend may not call you to tell you about the gorgeous bird she saw while getting into her car, but if a bird pooped on her head, you'd hear all about it.

What's more, we are hard on ourselves. Women do absolutely extraordinary things all the time, but we often don't see ourselves as extraordinary. We focus on our failures rather than on our seeing all of our successes. It's time to refocus that negative lens and begin thinking about positive perspectives.

Take Action
Open Up to Your Own Wisdom

This exercise will help you learn from yourself and your experiences. Consider each of the following calls to action. You may even want to write your thoughts in your B.A.L.A.N.C.E. Journal.

1. **Spotlight yourself.** Think about you as your best self, when you are fully engaged and plugged in to life. You may remember a specific situation or an overall feeling. Envision it in a way that brings it back clearly and vividly for you.

2. **Recall an engaging experience.** What was your most powerful experience with your life, your health, your body, your self- esteem—a time when you felt most alive? What made it so energizing? Who was there? What surrounded you? Describe the specific experience in detail.

3. **Focus on what's working.** Identify areas of your life that are working well. Describe clear examples of past and present out-comes that you deem a success.

4. **Identify your strengths.** Women are amazingly strong. We juggle many things without even flinching. We help others without question. List some of your strengths and describe them in full detail.

5. **Unleash your can-do attitude.** Forget limitations. Let go of what you can't do. Challenge yourself to think in terms of what's possible, and what you can do. Acknowledge all you can do, all you can control, and don't give power to what you can't. Make a list of things you can start doing now to be your healthiest self.

Rekindle Your Power to Create

I remember once after a quick trip to the dollar store, my kids and I came home with modeling clay. We opened the box and got right to work on creating shapes. My son wanted to make a snowman with a hat, and my daughter set out to create an ice-cream cone with a cherry on top. Next we made a family, then a flower, a basketball, a birthday cake, and the alphabet. We molded and messed up and started again and mixed colors and created for hours on end. It was a blast.

Playing with modeling clay made me think how gratifying it is to create something. There's a joy that we get when we start from scratch—the song writer creating music, the builder constructing a home, the farmer growing vegetables, the artist molding a sculpture. I find more joy in baking a cake with eggs, flour, and sugar than with a box mix.

The modeling clay also made me think about the power we each have to create something out of nothing. Look at the highways where once there were dirt roads and, before that, just land. It is incredible. We all have that power, each with our own talents. When we combine our unique gifts with the power we have to create something, the sky really is the limit.

I always say limitless possibilities emerge with creativity and imagination. We are all born with this ability, but sometimes as we get older, our creativity is suppressed or we're taught to fit a mold that doesn't allow for imagination. And then we forget what makes us come alive.

It is so important, though, to question ourselves so we remember what our gifts are and so we use them to serve the world. I've witnessed the power of imagination and creativity in my own life as well as in the lives of many of my friends, family members, and clients. This is key to being filled with passion and energy, to being our most joyful selves.

As you travel on your balance journey, think about rekindling your dormant creativity and imagination. Think about ways you can be creative and express your talents. How can you be creative even in areas where you think you have no talent? Even if you can't draw a straight line (I definitely can't!!), you may still have fun sketching, crafting, or painting. Once you let go of feelings of limitation, fear, and worry, there's no end to what you can create.

Create Your Revived Life Vision

Without leaps of imagination, or dreaming, we lose the excitement of possibilities. Dreaming, after all, is a form of planning.
—Gloria Steinem

Vision. This is one of the most common elements for actualization of our dreams. Vision allows you to see clearly from your heart into your mind's eye, watching it like a movie. Vision is what guides you beyond the past and moving toward the future.
Tucked away in each of us is a dream, a purpose, something we were born to do to serve the world. But in order to dream while we are awake, we must revive our life vision, really look within, take the dream out of hiding, and give it power by visualizing it in living color.

Creating a revived vision for yourself is the foundation to making any kind of change in your life. If you don't have a vision, you won't know where you're going—it's like planning to meet a dear friend for lunch without knowing exactly where she is waiting for you. You may never find her. To better understand yourself, you need to take some time to uncover truths that you may have forgotten. Careful questioning helps you rediscover who you are and remember your awesomeness.

To create your vision, you have to look into your heart and use your mind's eye to visualize what your dream really looks like. You have to feel it with every fiber of your being. You have to see it so much that you believe it is happening now.

Many women laugh when I first describe the concept of vision. One woman even shouted during class, "I just want to see myself thinner!" I heard her loud and clear, so I asked the group, "if I waved a magic wand, and poof you were thinner, would the weight loss alone really make you feel happy and fulfilled?" Of course, their answer was a resounding no.

From my personal experience (and having worked with thousands of women), I know that weight loss does not solely equate to joy, health, happiness, fulfillment, or success. As a matter of fact, I can't define what success in life means to you. Only you can determine that for yourself. I've chased the holy grail of a size 4, I've been there, but when I got there, I chased for the holy grail of a boyfriend, the holy grail of a pair of shoes, the holy grail of a career.

Chasing for external happiness was just that: a never-ending chase. I set out to explore what truly can create a life of joy, health, happiness, and balance . . . my conclusion was simply this: it comes from lighting that spirit within ourselves, contributing to the world, showing up for it. It begins with love of humanity, love of self, and with vision, faith, intention, and purposeful action.

Dig deep when visioning, tap into the joy you want to feel with every fiber of your being. See yourself living the best version of your life possible as a passionate, vibrant version of yourself. Steps and goals are all well and good, but if you're not pulling your vision from a deep, personal place, the steps will get you nowhere. I believe the vision often lends itself to creating the steps naturally, and it doesn't feel like exhausting work, but rather an exciting movement forward.

Studies show that 86 percent of women feel most beautiful when they are fulfilled and happy in their lives. My guess is that you may have picked up this book because you not only want to find balance, but you also want to feel excited to be alive. You want to feel amazing about getting up in the morning, taking care of your family, going to work, spending time with good friends, having fun, being creative, and glowing with emotional, physical, and spiritual health. You want to have the energy to do things that bring joy and happiness.

Take Action
Create a Purpose Statement for Your Life

To do this, you must release all boundaries, obstacles, fears, and limiting beliefs from your mind. Without limitation, close your eyes and see a detailed vision for your life. Picture yourself, your attitude, your temper, your demeanor. Hear yourself speak. Watch yourself move. What is your life like? Describe your relationships, your home, your family life, your career, your fun. Be as detailed and specific as possible. Have fun. Imagine moments. Use your talents. Help others with them. See yourself at work—contributing, being heard, sharing. Picture your body in motion and working to its full capacity, pushing yourself beyond your comfort zone. Imagine food as your energizer and feel yourself enjoying the taste, texture, and flavor of natural, fresh, vibrantly colored foods. Imagine yourself living a life that is in full balance with your core values.

In your B.A.L.A.N.C.E. Journal, describe your purpose statement in full detail. I strongly believe that we must be the cocreator of our lives, and that means knowing exactly how we want our lives to look, feel, and be. It's empowering to make the choice to live on purpose.

This activity isn't very structured. It's kind of your free space to bust open your dream and let it out. Ideally you'll be smiling the whole time during this activity because your vision should make you happy. If it stresses you out, it's not the right life vision for you.

Bear in mind, purpose presents itself in so many ways, it is not an absolute, but rather fluid. God uses us in ways we just can't even imagine, but asking him to use us is a beautiful invitation for God to take the wheel of our lives and release the burden from ourselves.

Here are some other ways to think about your purpose statement:

Find a quiet space so you can dream while awake. This is an incredible experience (and a blast too!). It allows you to release all boundaries, walls, and obstacles. Picture in color and motion what you are doing. Begin with your personal life—family, home life, the way your space is decorated, the things you do for fun, what you are passionate about, how you maintain an active lifestyle. Next, move into your career or professional life. Picture your office space, see what you are doing, and feel the positive impact you are making.

Remember, we are acting as if. We are not worrying about the how—it does not matter right now. There are no boundaries. No rules. You are defining your success. What is your overall philosophy on life?

Key note: Dreaming while you are awake is not about daydreaming. Remember, there are certain nonnegotiables in your life, and if you are daydreaming about something that simply cannot hap- pen because of one of your nonnegotiables, you are wasting your energy, and you'll always feel unfilled. Make sure your dream aligns with your core values.

Next: Imagine that anything you desire has come to be and that you are living exactly the life you've envisioned.

Create a "purpose-filled" vision collage. Using a board, wall, box, book, or space of any kind (digital or physical) start to gather images of anything and everything you find pleasing at the core that align with those values you uncovered earlier. Be creative! You can clip photos or words out of magazines and newspapers, take photographs, or find color swatches of paint.

Now, I say "purpose-filled" vision because over the years I've seen many vision boards that include material items like cars or a large diamond ring. I understand, of course, these may be things that you find exciting! For this activity, try to find clippings that encapsulate a deep feeling of purpose, peace, or the fruits of the spirit love, joy, peace, patience, kindness, goodness, faithfulness, gentleness and self-control. This vision board should stir your soul, and shift your being picture by picture, clip by clip.

You can turn your dreaming into a written purpose statement, you can paste pictures in your journal and scrapbook your vision, or you can use a large board—the most important part is that you have a visual or written reminder of the purpose-filled vision that you just created in your mind.

If you like something tangible but the idea of a vision collage, board, or wall seems a little hokey, grab your favorite notebook or journal and begin a vision book.

Make and sign a commitment contract to yourself. Make a contract with yourself and commit to your vision statement or vision collage by writing a very simple one-line commitment pledge and signing off on it You deserve to live the best version of your life possible, so commit to it!

You can use something like this as a starting point:

I am committed to being present in my life, to being an active participant in my life, to taking footsteps toward the dream that is in my heart, to living on purpose, and to holding strong to my vision. I commit to living a healthy life, to nurturing my body as it is an instrument to using my gifts to serve the world, and to being a healthy example for everyone I care about in my life.

You can add your own personal details as they pop into your heart - it does not have to be all at once. You can add to it over days, weeks, months, years.

The beautiful thing is that with your openness, you have created a revived life vision and made a firm commitment to your extraordinary power. You began to shift your energy to focus on the awesome human being you are today. Being in balance from within begins with deep gratitude for who you are in this very moment.

B.A.L.A.N.C.E. Technique #2:
Connecting with Our Breath

There are times when no matter how calm you try to be, no matter how much you brain dump, your mind still swirls. You will be busy, frantic, running, concerned, worried, and stressed. This is life, we are human, and it happens. There will be situations we cannot control. We will make mistakes. We will fail.

Even during the most chaotic, stressful times in your life, you can use simple tools to help clear your mind and feel lighter and calmer. I identified these B.A.L.A.N.C.E Techniques while dealing with my own very personal, very difficult situations.

When something is weighing heavy on me, I simply connect with my breath. Breathing in and out, slowly and mindfully, I let go of regrets about the past and apprehension about the future. This connection is pure light. You will love the way it feels. Give yourself permission just to "be" by breathing. Come as you are, and release with your breath, that which gives you life literally, gives you life spiritually as well.

Everyone breathes—we die if we don't. But most of us don't breathe properly. We take shallow breaths and take in just enough oxygen to get by. That's automatic breathing. Add mindfulness, and breathing delivers so much more.

Mindful breathing is deep. When you breathe deeply, you send extra oxygen to your brain and the cells of your body. Actual biochemical changes occur in your body right away. You feel more relaxed because your body immediately begins to produce lower levels of the stress hormones, such as cortisol, that rev you up and can make you feel nervous.

Mindful breathing can lower your heart rate, blood pressure, and muscle tension; boost your mood by reducing anxiety and feelings of depression; and facilitate healthy digestion.

Begin to notice the way you breathe. Like many of my clients, you'll probably notice that you hold your breath a lot. Yawning, sighing, and feelings of fogginess and fatigue are signs that you're not getting enough oxygen.

Take Action
Practice Mindful Breathing

Mindful breathing—also known as diaphragmatic breathing or belly breathing—is a skill that you can learn with a bit of practice.

Over time, it can become second nature. Here's how to do it:

1. Inhale deeply and slowly through your nose. As you inhale, allow your lungs to fill and your belly to expand to make room for all the air you're taking in. Hold the air in your lungs for a few seconds to give your lungs time to absorb oxygen and to let your body relax.

2. Slowly exhale through your mouth. Use your abdominal muscles to help your diaphragm push the air out of your chest.

3. Repeat several times.

Chapter Two - B is for Brain Dump and Breathe

Practice mindful breathing a few times a day—when you get up, while you're stopped at traffic lights, before you go to bed, and so on.

A few years back my Little Man dropped our laptop. He tripped over Lulu's flip flop, and was totally fine, but unfortunately the laptop didn't fair so well. As you can imagine, there's a lot of important stuff on the laptop - all of our family photos, all of my work, and just a lot in general.

In the moment that I realized the laptop went kaput, I was chatting with a dear friend about a situation she was dealing with, and as I heard my own voice begin to escalate in response to her issue, I knew I had to release the stress myself or else I would project it through the rest of our conversation.

I took a deep breath in, then exhaled slowly. "I'm sorry, Vanessa. My laptop just went, it's completely fried. Guess it's God's way of clearing out the hard drive to begin again, fresh..."

The breath calmed me immensely, and then as soon as I said the words, I felt better about the situation. I know if I go to a computer shop there's a chance they may be able to retrieve all of our stuff. Breathing it out and releasing it {both verbally and internally} helped ALOT. There have been times in my life, though, when I would have stifled it, saying on the outside "It's no big deal." But on the inside the stress never really left and would trigger me to act out less than healthy behaviors to cope - eat, shop, hold it all in, or project it on to other situations, people, things.

Now, I know this was just a laptop, and the situation could have totally been prevented {lesson learned for me}. But, there's no question, stressful things come in many forms, and happen to us all. If we don't choose how we want to release the stress - our triggers will train us or drain us. We need to choose how we want to respond, and retrain our triggers.

Choosing an alternate stress response was one of the first things I did, once I understood how I was handling stress and realized it wasn't serving me {or others} well.

Here are a couple of questions for you to consider:
1. How do you handle stress? When a "stressful" situation happens, what is your response? Do you hold it in until you're going to burst? Or, do you unconsciously "stress eat"

or "stress shop" or "stress spend"? Do you project your stress onto others by yelling, snapping, or by being overly critical? Be honest with yourself, this is not about judgment {remember self-discovery should be a Judgment-Free Zone}, it's about awareness. We can't change what we are unaware of, so just knowing how you respond to stress beings a level of awareness that is necessary for movement forward in a healthy way.

2. How would you prefer to handle stress? What is a healthy behavior that you can choose to do in response to stress? How will you remind yourself of your healthy stress-response choice until it becomes learned?

Now, I'm sure you've heard the phrase "don't sweat the small stuff" - sounds simple, but I realize how hard it can be. I get it, I've stressed out about things both big and small - over the years, strengthening my faith became integral.

The amount of time you spend feeling and experiencing stress is directly correlated to overall health, as almost every organ in the body is affected negatively by stress. And whenever you're feeling stressed, overwhelmed, anxious, worried, or upset, take a few moments to breathe mindfully. You will soon feel calmer and better able to cope with whatever is bothering you.

Summing up

In this chapter, we've discussed the benefits of brain dumping as well as some great ways to empty your mind of clutter. We've also looked at the benefits of breathing deeply and mindfully. The activities I suggested include:
- Do a free-form brain dump to move worrisome thoughts from your brain to your B.A.L.A.N.C.E Journal.
- Do an exercise that will help you center your focus on your strengths, your abilities, and your past successes to discover your strongest self.
- Use what you've learned in your brain dump to create a revived life vision and a purpose-filled vision statement for your life.
- Eat mind-clarifying foods that are rich sources of vitamin c, vitamin e, B vitamins, and iron.
- Practice deep breathing, which reduces feelings of stress and calms your anxious mind.

Chapter Two - B is for Brain Dump and Breathe

In chapter 3, I'll share some assessment tools that will help you look honestly and completely at your life as it is now so you'll have the knowledge you need to move toward where you want to be.

Chapter Three
A is for Assess and Accept

Awareness is like the sun. When it shines on things, they are transformed. - Thich Nhat Hanh

Once when I was driving to an event in an unfamiliar neighborhood, I thought I knew where I was going, but it seemed like I had been driving in circles for twenty minutes. Finally I called the venue to ask for directions. I told them I was a bit lost, so naturally the first question they asked me was, "Where are you now?" I looked at a street sign and told them the name, but I didn't know if I was north- or southbound on the street, I wasn't even sure what town I was in, and I couldn't identify a landmark because I was in a residential neighborhood.

The woman on the phone couldn't help me. "I'm sorry, dear. I can't tell you where to go if you don't know where you are. Find out and call me back."

The same is true for life. Living and knowing the truth of who you are in this moment, and assessing and accepting the woman you are, opens you up to being the woman you were born to be.

Honoring our core values brings us back to a place of loving ourselves. We all have talents that sometimes we aren't fully utilizing, but with a little dusting off, we can bring them back to life, so we can live with passion and energy, serve others, and live our purpose.

Continually facing my truth allows me to stretch and grow to, and I am sure as you face yours, you will feel the same way.

Chapter Three - A is for Assess and Accept

In this chapter, I'll help you assess your life as it is now, so you'll have the information you need to open up to your awesomeness, even more so than you already have!

B.A.L.A.N.C.E Technique #3
Assess: So You Know Who You Are and What You Stand For...

Assessing is all about self-discovery, about taking a clear, honest look at your current situation and your true self in order to create your own meaning and method for balance. Your method must align with who you are as a person, your core values, and what's important in your life. If these aspects aren't factored in, you will feel like you are doing rather than being – just going through the motions rather than actually living a balanced life that aligns with your unique personality.

In order to create and reach your goals, you've got to take an introspective look at who you are and what you truly value, meanwhile rediscovering who you were born to be. Accepting your own reality and understanding that true awakening takes work (and personal responsibility) are key to moving forward.

So to find balance from within, assess these key areas:

1. Your body—including your strength, physical structure, health, and physical energy source (food)

2. Your internal muscle—including your core values and mental energy source (attitude)

3. Your caring balance—the delicate balance of how you care for others vs. how you care for yourself

4. Your schedule—including your lifestyle factors and the way you use time, because the busyness of your life can have a huge impact on your ability to be in balance

5. Your anime vs. animus, this is your masculine vs. feminine sides - we will look at the balance of 'being' (looking at the stars, smelling the roses, in the moment) vs. 'doing' (setting alarms, go-go-going).

Below, there's a nifty graphic that shows you (in a nutshell), the areas that affect our overall sense of balance and love of self.

In the center, you'll notice are the core values. These will serve as both your anchor to keep you centered regardless of life circumstances, and your compass to guide you through life.

Your physical body and your internal muscle combined create your overall strength. Having strength creates the confidence necessary to move forward with your vision, believe in yourself, and use your gifts to serve the world.
Your lifestyle factors create your schedule. An overall sense of being in balance combines your overall strength with your lifestyle factors and caring balance.

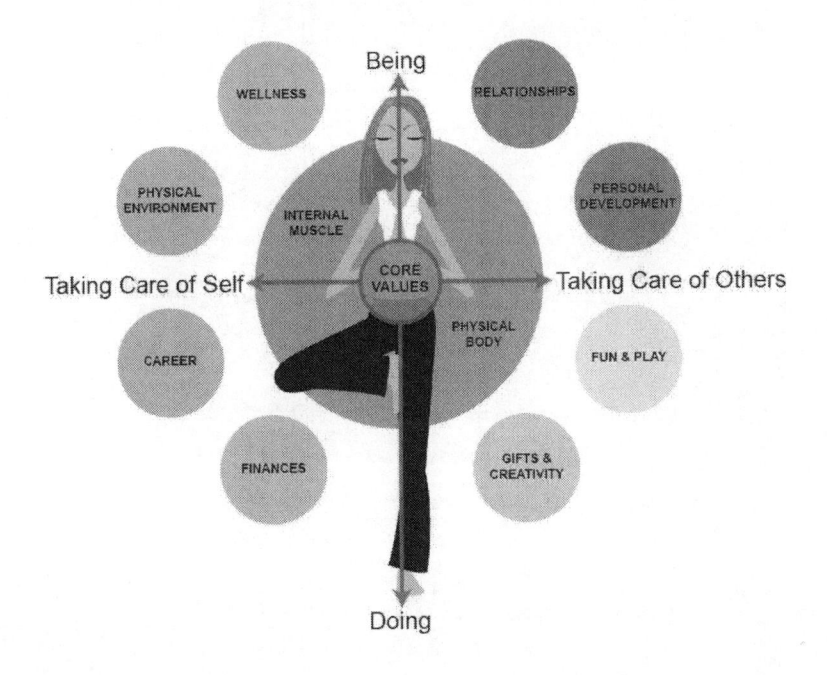

Diagram: A figure in a yoga tree pose at the center, surrounded by labeled circles. Vertical axis: Being (top) ↔ Doing (bottom). Horizontal axis: Taking Care of Self (left) ↔ Taking Care of Others (right). Center: CORE VALUES. Inner labels: INTERNAL MUSCLE, PHYSICAL BODY. Outer circles: WELLNESS, RELATIONSHIPS, PHYSICAL ENVIRONMENT, PERSONAL DEVELOPMENT, CAREER, FUN & PLAY, FINANCES, GIFTS & CREATIVITY.

Use your B.A.L.A.N.C.E Journal to assess your current state in the areas identified in the graphic.

Chapter Three - A is for Assess and Accept

Assessing Your Body

How do you feel about your body? Back when my self-image was completely out of balance, I didn't like my body, and the less I had to look at it, the better. But once I learned to love and accept myself, my appreciation for my body deepened. Taking the very important first step of assessing and accepting my body paved the way for me to nurture it in a variety of healthy ways.

We have to develop a relationship with ourselves, and doing a body assessment is a way we get to know ourselves. I can't tell you how many women simply have no clue about their physical, cardiovascular, or muscular endurance. The first step toward change in any aspect of our lives is recognizing, acknowledging, and accepting what is —then we are ready to take ourselves to the next level and move forward.

As opposed to being critical of your body, assessment is a means to grow deeper in gratitude for your body. Often when a woman completes a body assessment, she is amazed and inspired by her own strength. By assessing your body, you are actually reconnecting with it! And, this reconnection allows you to start releasing judgment and accepting your body as it is in the present moment. Accepting is a precursor to self-love and self-nurturing.

Believe it or not, I find that most women do not see themselves the way they actually are or as others see them, and they generally have a very skewed self-image. They nitpick and focus on what they think are the flawed areas rather than the overall image of the beautiful, unique, amazing women that others see.

Take Action
Do Your Own Body Assessment

In your B.A.L.A.N.C.E. Journal, create a page that looks like this:

Date:

Measurements:
    Chest/Back
    Waist
    Abdomen
    Hips
    Thighs
    Arms

Calves

Weight:

Pain Issues:
    Where   How Often   Intensity

10-second heart rate:
    Resting
    (beats of your pulse when you are sitting still)
    Active
    (beats of your pulse after doing 30 seconds of jumping jacks)

Assessing Your Health

I know having borderline diabetes was certainly my wake-up call, and many clients come to me when they feel their health is at risk. If you haven't had a full physical lately, now is a good time to make an appointment so you can find out your current blood pressure, blood sugar, cholesterol levels, and so forth.

Be honest with yourself and your doctor about any health symptoms, early warning signs, or risk factors. If you have a family history of heart disease, diabetes, high cholesterol, or cancer, make a note of it. Preparing a list of these risks as well as your questions for your doctor is the best way to get the most out of your appointment. Knowing your current state of health will help you when you are figuring out the healthiest food choices for you. You have the power to overcome many health problems by changing your lifestyle.

Assessing Your Physical Nourishment

In the following section, we'll assess the foods you use for fuel and identify their effect on your mind and body.

Take Action
What's your Food-Mood Connection?

Food can have a profound effect on your mood and your attitude. It causes a chemical reaction that can make you feel happy or sad, connected or distant, tired or energized. Certain foods can amplify feelings of anxiety and stress; others can calm you. They can also affect your brain function and your cognitive awareness.

You're probably wondering which foods will make you feel good—I'm sure you'd like a list of them so you can eat them every day!

But the food-mood connection is different for everyone. A food such as oatmeal, which makes me feel great, may do nothing for you. And something like raisins, which leave me feeling tired and heavy, may be just the energetic pick-me-up that can fuel you through a long afternoon. So it's up to you to observe the effects of various foods on you and, through trial and error, to figure out what belongs on your plate. And remember that combinations count. Sometimes it's a combination of foods that affects you, so if you're feeling sluggish, look beyond individual foods.

To tease out the effects of various foods on your mood and attitude, keep a food-life inventory for about a week. Create a Food Assessment worksheet in your B.A.L.A.N.C.E. Journal. Write down all the foods you eat, along with the time you ate them, your moods throughout the day, your movement, and what's going on in your life.

Begin noticing how different types of foods make you feel. You'll probably discover that some foods make you feel good and others leave you sluggish and tired. That's important information for you to know as you create your own best balanced diet.

As you go along, scribble down any observations you may have about possible food-mood connections. If you notice that you feel great all morning when you have granola and fruit for breakfast but exhausted at ten a.m. when you breakfast on a bagel and jam, write it down. Then try both breakfasts again and see if the observations hold up. Continue to experiment with all the foods you commonly eat.

Make sure to hold on to this worksheet—we'll be referring back to it in Chapter 4.

Identifying Your Triggers

We all have trigger foods—treats like chocolate or cheese or salty chips—that we can't stop eating once we start. Say you're triggered by chocolate chip cookies. One small cookie may turn you into the cookie monster and create a binge that can last for weeks.

For some people, certain foods can be addicting.

Use your food assessment Worksheet to help identify your trigger foods and decide whether there are foods you should avoid completely—

Just as a recovering alcoholic has to stay away from liquor and a former smoker avoids cigarettes, knowing your trigger foods and facing up to the power they hold over you will help you as you set out to balance your eating behaviors.

You may also have trigger moments—out-of-balance situations that send you running for the refrigerator in an attempt to cope with stress, exhaustion, or worry. The food assessment Worksheet can also help you identify trigger moments and create plans to help you handle them in ways that will pave the way for you to feel calmer, lighter, and less likely to head for the kitchen.

What are You Eating?

Being aware of what you are eating matters because you may discover that you are over- or under-fueling your body, taking in low-quality fuel, or fueling your body for reasons way deeper than physical hunger.

Create a worksheet in your B.A.L.A.N.C.E journal like the one on the next page. Leave space to write both what you eat and a bit about your mood. Some of my clients even use "emojis" to show mood quickly and easily. This is by you and for you, so you can complete it any way you see fit that is helpful to identifying your FOOD-MOOD connections.

Chapter Three - A is for Assess and Accept

WHERE DOES YOUR "PHYSICAL FUEL" COME FROM?
ASSESS IT!

Physical Fuel is the food you take in to support mood, attitude, and energy! *Fuel your body on things that truly nurture and nourish you!*

Food/Mood/Attitude Log

	Breakfast	Mid-Morning	Lunch	Mid-Afternoon	Dinner
Monday					
Tuesday					
Wednesday					
Thursday					
Friday					
Saturday					
Sunday					

Some Assessment Tips:

In order to assess yourself, you must be in a calm, cool, collected sort of state. Assessing is about accepting who you are now, so as you work on this chapter, consider adding some nutrients that have soothing benefits to create calm in your life:

Make a soothing spread: Peel back an avocado and mash it up. Chop in some tomatoes, a sprinkle of sea salt and pepper, and then spread it on crackers, toast, or tortillas. The potassium in tomatoes and avocados will help soothe you.

Create a calming mix: Combine dark, leafy greens such as chard with chopped artichoke and chopped egg whites to create a salad mix full of calming B vitamins and magnesium. These nutrients help convert the amino acid tryptophan, which is found in egg whites, into serotonin, a brain chemical that helps your body calm down, unwind, and relax.

Take time for tea: L-theanine, a compound found in tea leaves, is thought to promote relaxation and enhance mood by stimulating the production of alpha brain waves. Tea (especially green tea) also contains compounds that may help reduce blood pressure, prevent hypertension, and rev up metabolism.

Assessing Your Internal Muscle

Transformation is often simply a perspective shift, that can happen in a moment. It absolutely begins within your heart, followed by allowing your heart to fuel your mind. Your attitude, the way you process information, and your core values all create your internal muscle. Just like physical muscles, the internal muscle needs to be worked out, stretched, and practiced daily. Assess your internal muscle, particularly:

Core values: using your core values from chapter 2, write a list of ways you currently honor each of them. For example, if a core value is giving and you tithe, note it here.

Internal strength: list all the sources of internal strengthening that you currently partake in or have experienced within the last three months, along with the date or time frame. Also note if it has had a positive, negative, or neutral effect on you.

Some examples are seeing a coach, counselor, therapist, or business advisor; partaking in online or in-person communities, contributing to your community by volunteering your time, collecting needed items for a local shelter, beginning a garden to feed people in need, donating your gently used items, educating someone on a topic you are very knowledgeable on, and so forth.

If you feel fulfillment, healing, support, or forward movement, the activity has a positive effect. If you feel con- fused, frustrated, empty, or angry, it probably has a negative effect on you. And if you simply don't know or you feel like it's a take-it-or-leave-it activity, call it a neutral. Also add any notes that come to mind while assessing these activities.

Slowing Down the Speed of Life

A couple years back, I went to the store to pick up a few things we needed for the house. I went to the express lane for people with 15 items and under, and there was a short line. The woman in front of me had all of her items on the conveyer belt, but the man who was checking out was having an issue with a price, causing a slight delay in moving forward.

When he opted to actually write a check as opposed to swipe his debit card, the woman in front of me nearly exploded. She grabbed all of her items and carried them to the next lane which looked like it was moving faster. I loaded my items on the belt, and in seconds the man's check was written, he was out the door, and I was being rung up.

The woman who left the line was still waiting; apparently there was an issue at the register she switched to. I felt bad as I walked passed her, and could hear her distress, so I just gave her an empathetic smile and left.

Two days later I was pulling into the bank parking lot. As I pulled my car into the spot, another car zoomed into the lot and pulled through my spot (from the other side). The woman in the racing car didn't see me pulling into the spot. Rather than cause a raucous, I opted to simply back out and pull into another space. The lot was empty after all.

The woman ran into the bank and I was behind her. She had to stop to speak with the bank manager, so I went into the teller line. A few moments later, the woman finished her conversation and entered the line, too.

Again, it wasn't moving as quickly as the woman behind me would have liked. I could feel her impatience huffing on my back, so I turned to try to 'break the ice' with a smile, and strike up a conversation to make the time move faster. She wasn't into it, and that was ok. I understood.

At that moment, the woman huffed out of the line and went out to the ATM to finish her banking. Immediately after she left, the teller opened up, quickly finished my deposit, and went on to the next customer. As I left the bank, the woman was still fiddling around with the ATM furiously.

Wow. I received the same message just 2 days apart.

There are no shortcuts. Patience pays off. There is no 'easy way'. If you try to buck the system, you will end up still standing at the ATM.

What's the lesson that I'm supposed to learn?

God has his own watch, and if we stay in faith, be patient with where He's placed us, don't move to an option that seems 'quicker, don't avoid the pain of the situation to take the path of least resistance, eventually the 'line' will open up and we will move forward.

But, patience isn't the easiest thing for any of us, especially since time is funny.

We are all on our own schedules, I guess, but in reality we have little to no control over time vanishing. It moves as it should, not sure if it's fast or slow, or if the speed of life is relative to how plugged into time we are.

If we're rushing through it, time travels fast. If we're "waiting" for the next thing, it feels like we're stuck, which leads to impatience with our current situation. But, if we're "in" it, truly absorbed in each moment of our lives, time simply moves from one moment to the next, and then it's gone.

I know many people (I've been one of them myself) who have schedules packed from morning until night, without even a moment to just breathe. But, after I had my daughter, I noticed something --

Chapter Three - A is for Assess and Accept

she was "plugged in" to time, to life. No matter what she was doing, even when she was drinking her bottle, she was connected to it. She experienced the moment. She experienced every moment. My son is just the same. He is fully engaged in whatever he is doing.

In seeing the world through my children's eyes, a profound lesson emerged -- the beauty is in every second, when we are actually experiencing time. Sometimes we don't even realize that the hectic schedule (that we fight hard to adhere to) is actually the very thing that can completely throw off us from living to our pure potential.

I think how we schedule our lives is actually a test of our faith.

We hear a lot about time, scheduling, time management, but, I don't believe time should be managed, because when we try to manage time, we can always find a way to fit more stuff in. And many of us do just that: we manage time, we squeeze in more and more and more responsibilities until we're so stuffed we literally burst.

And it's not until that breaking point that we realize, time should not be managed after all.

Navigating life is not a science of learning how to juggle more and better and faster. Rather, it's about doing less. It's about taking a good hard look at how we spend time and making choices about whether or not we want to continue to spend time in this way. It's about delegating, asking for help. It's about saying, "No" to some things and "Yes!" to others.

It's about prioritizing and arranging our day, and eliminating those wasteful 'time vacuums' so we don't inadvertently get pulled into something that we don't need.

Time is about choice. Choice is freeing.

And the choice is ours. We can set our own terms, and we don't need to get caught up in the "mad rush". Even when we know something must give, it's easy to keep thinking "next week, next month, next year will be better, will be slower". And so, we keep going. Sometimes it's a jolting situation that sends us running back into appreciation of life. Sometimes, it's simply knowing that there is too much is at stake -- our relationships, our health, our lives.

Time is a gift, and how we choose to spend our time is our love letter back to it, our 'thank you note', our appreciation of this miraculous, wonderful present.

I ask myself, "Do you believe it? Do you know it with every fiber of your being? Do you realize that time really is precious, that moments pass, and if you're not plugged into them, you may miss them forever?"

And then, I remind myself...

The moment that your niece tells you about her friend on the playground - savor it.

The moment that you take the first sip out of your morning coffee - taste it.

The moment that your neighbor tells you a story about his lawn - enjoy it.

If my schedule is too packed, I may miss these moments entirely. Yes, how we schedule our lives is a test of our faith, but many of us don't want to take that test.

I've heard all the reasons why it's impossible - I've thought about them all myself. I'm not judging; I think we all at some point fall victim to being the thieves of our own lives - stealing the joy, the beauty, the miracle from ourselves in order to run the rat race.

I try to take my running shoes off, and walk barefoot in the grass. I love life with less running, dashing, juggling. But sometimes, it happens. I rush. And then I try to correct it - I wonder if ever it was too late? I'm certain there were times I rushed so much, I missed the fact that I hurt someone, didn't look them in the eye, didn't really listen well. And the moment is gone, the feelings are not, and sadly, I may never know all the times I left wreckage behind in my rushing. Time is not a renewable resource after all. So I try, I try to rush less and (hopefully) have less to correct afterward.

I mean, I think it's just wonderful to bake a loaf of fresh bread, walk it over to our neighbors, and sit down to actually eat it together. To me, this is living. These are the memories, the tiny threads of experience that weave us all together as humanity.

Chapter Three - A is for Assess and Accept

Assessing Your Schedule

Is a frantic schedule preventing you from living a balanced life? Are you so busy working, taking care of other people, and keeping up with all your personal and professional responsibilities that you don't have time to eat well, exercise, nurture yourself, spend time with friends and family, go to church, volunteer your time, help others from your heart, and enjoy your life?

I remember once thinking that time had to be managed and that this meant squeezing more tasks into less time—balancing your checkbook while gulping down dinner, loading the dishwasher you talk to your mom on the phone, doing conference calls while you're driving your kids to soccer practice, or learning Spanish while running on the treadmill. But that's not a balanced approach, and it may even lead to less appreciation for life. As I mentioned, utilizing time in a balanced way is not about learning how to juggle more, better, and faster.

Balancing your time means taking a good hard look at how you spend your time and making tough choices about how you really want to use the minutes, hours, and days of your life.

It's about asking for help and delegating responsibilities, learning to say no, saying yes with mindfulness, grouping tasks into efficient bundles, and rearranging your schedule according to your most important priorities. It means putting the joy of life first and adding in tasks rather than trying to squeeze joy into the tiny bits of empty space in your calendar.

When you learn the true value of your time and make the choice of how you want to spend it, you'll feel calmer and less stressed, your life will open up. You'll find time for that art class you've wanted to take, that movie you've been dying to see, the fishing trip your kids have wanted to go on, the food pantry you've been meaning to visit, and the date you and your husband have been planning for the past two years. By taking control of your schedule, you'll give yourself the gift of time.

Take action
Do a Day Dump

The first step to balancing your time is becoming conscious of what you do every day. The Day Dump Worksheet is a great tool for this task.

Pour yourself a cup of coffee, tea, or water with lemon. Gather up a pen and paper (or if you prefer, a computer with a spreadsheet program), all your scheduling tools (day planner, calendar, smart phone, online calendar, and so on), along with four markers (red, green, blue, and pink). Find a quiet space where you can concentrate.

On your paper or spreadsheet, create eight columns. Label them with the seven days of the week. Label the eighth column miscellaneous.

Next, start writing. Begin to list everything you do every day for 1 week, from morning till night. Include even the most mundane tasks, such as brushing your teeth and tying your kids' shoes. Write down the time you spend surfing the web, scrolling your social media feeds. Write the time you are on the phone, or running to pick up stuff from the food store. Write it all down. The more specific you can be, the better, because little things can take much more time than you realize.

You may want to take a look at the Balanced Inspirista graphic at the beginning of the chapter—the little outer circles are the lifestyle factors. When you're doing your day dump, remember to factor in everything you do in all areas of your life.

When you finish the week, take a look at your lists. You will probably be amazed to see how much you do every day and to see it all written down in black and white. No wonder you feel so exhausted—you're probably doing the work of two or three women! No wonder you don't have time to take good care of your body.

Now grab your colored markers. It's time to start paring down your daily task load. Ask yourself these four questions:

1. Which of these tasks can I delegate? Grab your pink marker and highlight the tasks that someone else can do. Are you making lunches while your teens are playing video games? Are you folding laundry while your boyfriend is catching up on ESPN? Are you and your neighbor both driving to the same ballet classes and baseball practices? Are you giving your kids rides to places they can get to by foot or bicycle? At work, are you doing

jobs that could be done by coworkers? Are you making elaborate home-made dinners with friends when everyone would be just as happy with a potluck? Are you putting together the entire PTA bulletin board alone when other moms are able to help? I'm sure some mommies would love to contribute and cut out shapes while you staple the backdrop!

Delegating can be hard. You have to ask for help from people who may not be all that willing to chip in. You have to accept that others may not do the job as well as you would—for example, if your husband puts away the laundry, you have to accept that he may not share your feelings about the best way to fold a towel. If your kids unload the dishwasher, they may not stack the pots and pans in size order the way you do. But that's okay. What matters is that you have more time, not that your kitchen cabinets are arranged with military precision.

It may also surprise you how willing people are to chip in on the responsibilities, and (this will really shock you) they may even **want** to do stuff. They may even do things better than you do! I know when I first got married, I quickly found out that my husband was very good at some household chores, even better than I was. He was so used to doing things for himself, he enjoyed doing laundry and cleaning. Come to find out, he is a far better towel folder than I am, and he cleans corners like nobody else can. He's a regular old domesticated dad, and he loves it! Now, why would I take that joy away from him?

2. Which of these tasks can I group together? With your blue marker, highlight the tasks that can be grouped together to save time. Are there some things that you can clump together? For example, if you are spending too much time cooking and preparing lunches every day, consider doing a few days' worth of prep work on Sunday nights. Chop veggies, cook chicken, or freeze some casseroles, stews, or soups. You get the idea. This will free up morning time and evening time. Or do your workouts on your lunch hour instead of taking time at night or skipping the gym entirely. When you drop your daughter off at dance class, go food shopping and fill the car with gas to save time on the weekend. Clumping can make life easier if you do it in a way that works for you

If you prefer to have a little free time every night, clump less to spread out activities more. If you prefer having a few hectic days in order to have chunks of free time on other days, clump more. Do what makes the most sense for you.

3. Which of these tasks can I eliminate? Using your red pen, cross out the tasks that you no longer have to do (or want to do). If you're always the go-to gal for PTA event planning but are bored with baking for meeting nights, gracefully announce that you're no longer available for cupcake duty. If keeping your yard perfectly landscaped has become a chore, put away the clippers and let the yard look wild sometimes. If stopping for morning coffee adds fifteen minutes to your day, get out your Mr. Coffee and brew at home.

Eliminating can be even harder than delegating. It's so easy to look at a task and say, "I can't stop doing that!" But you can! I guarantee there are things on your daily to-do list that you can cut.

4. What are my priorities? Now, using your green pen, highlight the tasks that you can't eliminate, group, or delegate. These are the activities you want to do - remember time is about "choice". Remember your core values you assessed earlier in the book and do a "values check" - do my priorities align with and honor my core values? If not or if you're looking at the list and thinking, this really isn't a priority, find a way to eliminate, group, or delegate it.

We will use this activity in future sections, so sit tight and smile wide— we just assessed your time, and hopefully you have more of it already.

B.A.L.A.N.C.E. Technique:#4
Accepting it All

Flowers bring such joy into our world. I love flowers - they are beautiful, unique, awe-inspiring.

Flowers thrive by proper nurture and care, just enough sun and just enough water. But, it's funny, though, because if you look really close, the most beautiful flowers are flawed. If I were to pick apart the flowers petal by petal I would notice some perfect, shiny, bright

Chapter Three - A is for Assess and Accept

petals, and some crinkled, some a bit brown, some slighted wilted ones. I guess if a flower was just perfect with shiny, bright petals only it wouldn't be real - it would be synthetic.

This makes me think about people. Every human being is beautiful and every one of us is flawed, too. Collectively, our "layers" combine to create a unique, deep, real exquisite person. We function best when we take proper care of ourselves. But, even still, if we were to 'pick apart our petals', we would notice some aspects of our lives are wilted, a little brown.

If we choose to focus solely on the "brown petals", we may feel worthless and not want to nourish ourselves, share our gifts, or even show up in the world. We've all made mistakes, we all have life imperfections, but with continued care, we can blossom and thrive regardless.

What a lovely world it would be if we all chose to look at yourself (and others) without picking apart the petals. Notice the depth, the layers. Nurture yourself and others well, and soon you will only see the collective beauty of our humanity.

Situations and circumstances in life are often beyond our control. We make mistakes. We fall down. We will fail. We are human. I often used to spin my mental wheels when I was confronted with a difficult situation—a disagreement with a friend, a failed relationship, an empty bank account.

I even spent a number of years focusing mainly on my physical flaws— my dress size, the shape of my nose, the curl in my hair. I couldn't accept myself, and that caused me to waste so much mental energy. When I realized this, I decided to try to do a better job of accepting myself just as I am. Accepting became part of my everyday balance mantra, and it is much healthier than beating myself up over my flaws.

Accepting Situations or Circumstances

> *"Serenity is not freedom from the storm,*
> *but peace within the storm."*

I love this q; it has meant so quote, it has meant so much in my life. I have it posted on my refrigerator to serve as a way to keep me   grounded during turbulent times.

In a class I was teaching, I asked the ladies to name their most common cause of stress. One woman responded, "Stress comes from other people. People cause me stress." She then went on to list the various distressing things people had done to her. All were valid and beyond her control. Other top stressors included finances, lack of time, and impossible expectations.

Stress is hard to define—the dictionary lists ten meanings for the word. But too often we let stress define us.

What can you do if you have a daughter who is bulimic, a father who is an addict, a friend who doesn't seem to care about you, or a boss who keeps piling work on? Do you disown your family and friends, quit your job, and move to the nearest bubble? Hmm . . . Maybe you've felt like it, but it's obviously unrealistic, right?

We can often feel stressed even in less extreme scenarios. Try this one: your husband lost his job, you are two months late on your bills, your kids are in a million activities, and you have volunteered for one too many fund-raisers. You can't move to an island and seclude yourself from the realities of life. But there are some ways to find "peace within the storm," as the quote suggests.

Learning to Be Still

Stillness quiets the mind and centers you in the present moment. Although it takes some practice, stillness can give you a mental break from everything flowing through your brain—past worries, future concerns, and daily to-do lists. To practice stillness, find a space to just be —sitting under a tree in your yard, kneeling by the window, perched on your front step, soaking in a warm tub— whatever feels peaceful to you. Practice stillness regularly as a means of accepting. And remember, stillness includes listening. We may not know the answers, but sometimes when we listen, we hear the next step, or God provides peace in simply standing still.

Embracing Lessons

I've learned we have to detach ourselves from the problems and embrace them in the moment as an integral part of our lives. We usually think about the lesson after the problem has been resolved or enough time has passed for us to come to terms with it. Be open to the lesson. Show gratitude and always give yourself space for tears, venting, and acceptance. Be gentle with yourself and others.

Chapter Three - A is for Assess and Accept

Staying Connected

Detach from letting the situation define you and connect to the world around you. For example, if the economy is personally affecting you (as it is millions of Americans right now), you can still have fun with your family, dance around the room, watch a great movie, laugh, and say hi to a stranger. And if loved ones are struggling with something— illness, personal issues, a job loss— spend time with them, read together, reminisce, and create. Each moment carries perfection and imperfection—both are beautiful in their own right. Our circumstances should not stop us from loving life—it is a gift.

Take Action
Practice Acceptance

Sit down with your B.A.L.A.N.C.E. Journal and spend a few minutes writing about your perceived flaws and what you are working on accepting—physical imperfections, personality traits, or circumstances. Do you accept them, or do you waste energy wishing you could change the un- changeable? What flaw would you most like to learn to accept?

Of course, there's a difference between self-acceptance and plain old giving up. Each of us has to define our own acceptance standards.

Here is one of mine:
I accept that my hips are a bit wider since I had my children, but I won't use that as an excuse to feed my body junk. As long as I nurture, honor, and respect myself from the inside, meaning the way I fuel my body and the way I treat myself emotionally, I will accept how my physical body presents itself.

What are your acceptance standards?

My Acceptance Pledge to My Children

Back when my daughter was five, she asked me if she could begin ballet classes. This made me recall an incident in a coffee shop years ago when I overheard some mothers talking about ballet photos in front of their daughters.

One mother warned the other, "Make sure you pay the extra ten dollars to airbrush your daughter's flyaway hair and skin. I did my daughter's last year, and they came out amazing."

I was surprised to hear this, although I know that women are hard on themselves. It's difficult not to be with the impossible standards women have to deal with in magazines, on TV, and in the countless number of ways we believe we must be more perfect. But overhearing this conversation made me realize that these standards are now trickling down to children at younger and younger ages.

So I started to think about the pressures my daughter willwould be introduced to, very soon. I've always known that it's my job to give her a good, solid foundation of confidence and self-love from the inside out. I love every bit of her, and so should she. Even with my lu's wild mane of curly locks, flyaways galore, I couldn't imagine even wanting to airbrush them out. Honestly, aren't those the things we look back on with a smile?

I distinctly remember my first ballet photo. My hair was a bit of a mess and I didn't wear a drop of makeup. My mother was in the hospital, and she was the only one I would allow to do my makeup. "No Mommy, no makeup!" I said. I adored my mother, and I still do.

But loving our daughters is not enough. They have to see us love ourselves. Parenting happens best when we are being, not telling, doing, or saying. Experience is the greatest teacher. So if I am to stay true to setting a solid self-love foundation, I must always practice self-love. I must continue to be confident and strong. My daughter must not hear or see me pick myself apart, and in order to do that, I must simply not pick myself apart. I must love myself as I am.

This is my promise, my pledge to my daughter—and to my son too. Here are some of the things I must do to keep this pledge, which will teach them to love themselves and be the person they were each born to be.

I pledge to take care of myself. Moms need self-care too. This means eating well, moving our bodies, taking time for little indulgences (even as simple as a long, hot bath).

I work with thousands of women, and most of them do everything for everyone else and find very little time to practice self-care. Our self-worth is molded from the day we are born, and so is the self-worth our children develop. Daughters soon become mothers. If

Chapter Three - A is for Assess and Accept

we're constantly told we're not good enough the way we are, then we naturally begin to feel unworthy and we take less care of ourselves, which trickles to everyone else in our lives. Our children pick up this negativity. But if we feel fabulous, it helps everyone in the family feel fabulous. I will take care of myself so I can be the best mom and example to my children.

I pledge to put people above things. Success in my life means much more than a career or financial gains. Much of how I measure success is by love—how much I can give and receive. It's really all you need (as John Lennon said). But when we give of ourselves, we actually are giving to ourselves. We give ourselves a richness in spirit, a feeling of self-love and value. This leads to abundance in all areas of our lives. I want my children to be givers, to give to the world, to value our family and their friendships and strangers on The street. To teach them this, I will put people first above the material things. I will help others and lend a hand, an ear, spare change, or time. I will communicate. I will connect.

I pledge to love the flaws: mine, theirs, and everyone's. Home should be a safe place, where we can let our hair down, wash off our makeup, and just be ourselves, embraced for who we are as individuals. After all, our unique beauty is in our flaws—inside and out. I must love mine, I must love my children's, and I must love everyone's. If Lu or the Man see me being harsh on myself or others, they will in turn look at themselves harshly.

I pledge to live with passion, purpose, and intention. When we live with passion, purpose, and intention, then confidence just sits comfortably in our hearts. There is no trying to be confident. We just are. I have a purpose here on this earth. We all do. Sometimes we can get bogged down in the burden of finding our purpose, but I think it unfolds naturally when we live with passion. Purpose may evolve and change, and even if we don't know our purpose fully, we can be passionate about life and all its twists and turns. I will live with passion, believe in my purpose, and live with intention. Teaching this to my children is in and of itself one of the greatest gifts I can give them, as my parents gave to me.

I pledge to be a visionary and to follow through. When we have dreams, visions for our life that we put into motion, our confidence comes naturally from within. I know that many times, mothers and fathers put their dreams on hold to be caretakers. But I believe we must still have dreams and visions. I'm not talking about haphazardly chasing a crazy dream. I'm talking about using our natural talents, our unique gifts.

So, for me, this means I must take inspired actions and risks, and believe in my power. I must have faith. I must pray and meditate—speak to God and listen. This will teach my children that they can dream and achieve anything they want. Even when we reach small goals, we create small changes, and we enjoy a boost in confidence when we achieve bigger goals and create bigger changes.

I pledge to learn and to try again when I fail. Failure can be discouraging if we let it stop us, but it is necessary on the path of self-growth and teaching children self-worth. Whenever we fail, we have an amazing opportunity to learn and grow. When we believe in ourselves enough to try again, we are showing God we have faith, not just saying the words. I will teach my children that they can fly. But like a baby bird, they will fall a bunch of times, maybe even break a wing. Then eventually—with practice as well as failure, mistakes to learn from, and tenacity—they will soar.

Summing up

In this chapter, we've discussed the benefits of using self-assessment of your body, your mind, your self-care, and your schedule in order to find areas in your life that lack balance. I also suggested some strategies for acceptance. The activities I suggested included:

- Do a full assessment of your current state using the Balanced Inspirista graphic..

- Call your doctor and schedule a full physical.

- Do a day dump to help you clean out your schedule by pinpointing tasks that can be delegated, clumped, or eliminated.

- Create your acceptance standards and write an acceptance pledge to yourself or your loved ones.

In chapter 4, I'll guide you through a process of letting go of more unnecessary baggage, and I'll tell you how learning to say one tiny word can instantly add balance to your life.

Chapter Four
L is for
Let Go and Laugh

Sometimes you don't feel the weight of something you've been carrying until you feel the weight of its release... - Unknown

My husband loves to garden, so he knows that before he can plant anything, he's got to clear the ground—pull weeds, remove rocks, yank old roots, and rake away dead leaves and broken branches. Before new plants can grow, he's got to rid the garden of all the debris that might prevent vulnerable young seedlings from receiving the sunlight and rain they need to survive and thrive.

That's exactly what has to happen for us, we need to "empty" to "fill". Before you start making life-changing shifts and building exciting new habits, you've got to clear away physical and emotional debris so that as you plant the seeds of change, they have the space they need to grow.

I refer to this as a cleansing process because it is an opportunity to let go or get rid of some of the foods, thoughts, and behaviors that can be toxic to you as you implement the B.A.L.A.N.C.E techniques.

Letting go can feel liberating and exciting. It's a chance to eliminate what's no longer serving you or the greater good, or what doesn't align with and honor your core values in order to start fresh. It's a technique you can use throughout your life.

Technique #5
Let Go: To release what no longer serves you or the greater good.

The letting-go process is a comprehensive cleanse that will help you release the habits and out-of-balance life choices that have weighed you down for so long. It also signifies your commitment to yourself and to your awakening. It's very powerful to choose what you want to let go in order to become who you were born to be. You are making space for God to work through you.

As you begin, be sure you have your B.A.L.A.N.C.E. Journal by your side. Some of the activities you've done in previous chapters will help you determine what you need to release.

One important caveat before we start paring down: it's best to go through this process in a way that feels comfortable to you. The idea of a wholesale clearance is very scary to some people, and that's okay. If you're not the love-to-let-go type, start by simply reading this chapter, mulling over the recommendations, and applying them to you when and how you think would be best for you. But do keep in mind that the reason to go through a process of letting go is so you can make room to add important things enrich your life and the lives of others. After we finish letting go in this chapter, we'll begin adding in the next chapter.

You'll be surprised how light and free you'll feel once you start letting go.

As I began working with clients, I realized that many of them were holding on to behaviors that no longer served them well. In my personal life as well, I learned the importance of letting go in many ways—whether it came to food choices, relationships, thoughts, or even material possessions. Letting go is a powerful tool to make space for what's yet to come, and it became an integral part of the B.A.L.A.N.C.E techniques.

In this chapter, I'll guide you through a series of letting-go steps. First we'll go through a thorough cabinet and closet cutback in your home, clearing out the excess junk to determine what to donate, shred, repurpose, recycle, sell, or toss in the trash. Then we will figure out how to eliminate your time vacuums to help you let go of some of the things that unnecessarily suck time out of your life. Finally we'll do a mind-set purification to let go of self-limiting beliefs and unhealthy thoughts that are holding you back from

Chapter Four - L is for Let Go and Laugh

your awesomeness.

Remember the 3 R's When Letting Go

As you inherently know, you must release that which saps up or drains your power. We put up with, accept, take on, and are dragged down by people and situations that we may have come to ignore in our lives.

But the energy of throwing away or getting rid of things seems careless and not thoughtful. We are in a disposable world, I guess, but we can choose to lovingly let go of that which doesn't serve us or the greater good without just kicking it to the curb!

I use the 3 R's to determine whether to release, resolve, or restore power to them before just tossing it in the trash.

For example, if you are drained by a lot of physical clutter and old items that have nicks or scratches or tears, you may choose to release some of it (donate it), resolve it (create systems for organization), or restore power to old items by refurbishing them or repurposing them.

The same can be true for a relationship that may be draining you - you may choose to release it (is it time to move on?), resolve it (discuss root issues in a constructive way), or restore power to it (by reconnecting with meaningful talks, regular activities, listening, mirroring, etc.).

The Cabinet/Closet Cutback

Since everything carries energy and weight, and most of us spend a good portion of time in our homes, it's important to cleanse and detoxify your surroundings. This doesn't mean just throwing out the everything you keep under your sink—although that's not a bad idea to go through it. It means clearing out the unnecessary, expired, or junk food in your refrigerator and cabinets and cutting back on the clutter in your closets.

Go through your cabinets and refrigerator and determine what food to clear out. Immediately place it in bags or boxes to donate or throw away. It's up to you to define the meaning of the phrase junk food for yourself because it varies tremendously.

Once you've cleared the kitchen, go through (one by one) all of the closets, cabinets, and drawers in your home. Choose what to do with unnecessary items from the 3 R's discussed earlier - will you release them by donating gently used items or by recycling them, resolve storage issues to neaten the space, or refurbish old items to restore power to them?

Spring Cleaning Whatever the Season

Next, tackle the rest of your home with a thorough cleaning session. Dust the furniture, wash the windows, clean the bathrooms—I'm talking spring cleaning even if you're reading this in the dead of winter.

Cleaning your home from top to bottom is a kind of renewal—it allows you to start fresh. When you're scrubbing the stains out of the carpet, you're making a real commitment to your life. Cleaning out your home is a concrete, physical way to begin to clean out your life and allow God to use us in ways we just can't imagine.

If that sounds overwhelming, take baby steps. Begin with one section of your home, one room, even just one drawer. Even if you start small, the feeling you get from cleansing your home will extend into other parts of your life.

Redesign Your Life

Removing clutter can help you think more clearly: a Princeton University study recently found that visual clutter reduces your ability to focus and process information. Calmer energy, a sense of presence and balance, and sharper life focus can flourish in a decluttered home. Here are some simple ways to start cleansing clutter:

Set the stage. Go through your surroundings and take inventory. Is there a room that you aren't crazy about? Does it have wallpaper from the 1970s? A lightbulb that's not bright enough—or maybe a bit too bright? A hole in the wall? A squeaky door?

It doesn't cost much to put on a fresh coat of paint, fill holes, fix squeaks, and replace bulbs and batteries for a clean, updated look. And yet, it will make you feel so much better. And if design isn't your thing, flip through a magazine to find a picture of a room you love. Recreate the look yourself, and you'll save tons.

Chapter Four - L is for Let Go and Laugh

Choose colors carefully. Keep in mind that colors affect us more than we think. Pick colors that are conducive to what you want your space to be. If you want a serene room, stay away from red! Red is an energizer and may even stimulate your appetite. Greens are calming colors, perfect for a spa-inspired setting. Or if you want a cross between calm and amped up, choose a shade of blue.

Tackle your to-do list. We all have mental to-do lists, but now's the time to put it on paper and check it off. Make a list of the tasks that have been on your mind, like organizing a closet, filing cabinet, or drawer. Tackle the items one by one. Clearing clutter clears your mind too.

Store no more. Our closets, garages, and basements are havens for hidden treasures we may have written off too soon. You can go green and save green by refurbishing old furniture (it's amazing what furniture treatment and new hardware can do) or using bottles as decorative details (glass is said to be relaxing just to look through) to add a fresh new decor to your home. Be creative and you can design a whole new space with items you already own. Then cleanse your home and storage areas of what's not in use and no longer serves a purpose in your life.

Organize to organize. If you're trying to be organized, it may be overwhelming at first. Start simply by getting four bins and labeling them: Use, Donate, Toss, and Shred.

- Items in the "Use" bin should be put to use now!
- Donate items you no longer use by picking an organization of your choice. Many even offer free pickup services. Remember to clean them before donating!
- Toss whatever can't be used—either into the trash can or the recycling bin.
- Shred paperwork with private information and recycle it.

Eliminating Your Time Vacuums

In chapter 3, you used the Day Dump Worksheet to delegate and eliminate time-consuming activities from your schedule. But you may still find that you have less time than you'd like.

We've all had days that were perfectly planned out but, for some reason, nothing— I mean nothing—on our to-do lists gets done. If you're finding that every day is feeling like it's getting sucked away by unplanned tasks, you're probably getting stuck in a time vacuum. Eliminating time vacuums will free up space for healthier habits, such as dance class, volunteer activities, nature hikes, home cooking, healthy baking, or even at-home spa treatments. It will also lower the levels of stress hormones in your body.

So first check out your Day Dump Worksheet from chapter 3 and see what you are delegating and/or taking off of your to-do list. Hold yourself accountable to implement what you determined and have the conversations necessary to delegate.

Here are some other common time vacuums. Are they sucking away your time?

1. E-mail. E-mail is one of the worst time vacuums ever. Items just keep popping up in your inbox, demanding immediate attention. But you can take control by putting a few rules into place.
   - create a folder system within your inbox for messages awaiting a reply. Prioritize the categories and calculate a reasonable response time.
   - create standard replies to inform senders that they may be waiting to hear from you and include the expected wait time.
   - Delegate items when appropriate and delete junk or unsolicited nonessential items immediately. Don't waste time by checking out the latest dancing cat video, no matter how hilarious your friend promises it to be.
   - if you're using e-mail for personal messages or fun, you may want to designate a time of day for e-mails.
   - if you're anxiously awaiting something, you can use your phone to create an e-mail alert system so you don't always have to log in to the computer to find out if you've received the anticipated message.

2. Surfing the web. The internet has revolutionized the way we do business, find information, connect with friends, share pictures, and even shop. But sometimes you get so sucked in, you can't get out. To avoid wasting time on the web, view the internet as you would any other browsing activity. You wouldn't waste the day strolling around the mall when you are supposed to be at work. The same goes with the internet.

If staying off-line is particularly difficult for you, log on only during specific browsing times. Set a time limit and use an alarm to remind you when your time is up.

3. Talking on the phone. Who doesn't love a good girlfriend heart-to-heart? I know I do! But if you have a lot of friends and they call you often, those calls can suck up hours a day. I know—I've filled many days with long phone calls. But if the phone is interfering with your fulfillment, or your chatter is on a negative path, perhaps it's time to hang up. You can stay connected with your friends by beginning a purpose-filled project or activity together!

Learning to Say No

You may have to let go of some things on your to-do list. There's one thing standing between you and balancing your time: the word no.

If you feel like there just aren't enough hours in the day to do everything on your list, it's most likely because you say yes to too many people or activities!

My mother is notorious for being a yes-woman. She wants to help everybody all the time with everything, and she often puts herself to last on the list. I have to admit that when I was younger, I loved that my mother would drop everything to help people—especially me—but as I got older (and wiser, of course) I began to see that my mother was overextending herself. And I noticed I was doing it too! I was saying yes to everyone, and when I said no, I would spend days or weeks agonizing, feeling guilty, and apologizing.

I realized Mom and I were caught in an exhausting cycle: the Yes-No-Guilt-Exhaustion Cycle. I asked too much of her. She had trouble saying no to me, and when she did, I felt disappointed. This made her feel guilty. We had to stop this—I had to learn to ask for less, she had to get better at saying no, and we both needed to stop feeling guilty. Now, I remind her it's okay to say no when I ask her to watch my kids or support me in some other way. It's a good reminder that I have to say no more often too. Being aware, conscious, and considerate of her boundaries has opened me up to being more conscious of my own—and that's benefitted both of us.

There's no way to jam more hours in a day. The only way to free up time is to stop doing something—and the way to do that is to say no more often. Imagine yourself being pulled and stretched until you are almost unrecognizable—even elastic loses its "snap" at some point. Saying no will bring your life back into proportion.

Saying no is one of the most powerful ways to balance your schedule and your life. But no can also be one of the hardest words to say. It can make you feel selfish, negative, self-centered, uncaring, and guilty. Remember, if you're saying no to avoid something you simply don't have time for, you're not being selfish. Often we say "yes" because subconsciously we tie our worth to the things we do, the more we do the more valuable we feel. But what's the cost? If you can't properly commit, it's actually self-less, because you are making space for someone who may be ready and willing to take on the project.

If you can't think of a way to say no, you have some options. Here's an example: Your neighbor asks you to take care of her dog for a week while she's on vacation. This would involve feeding the dog and walking him two or three times a day. With your job, your own dog, your children, and the shelter you just volunteered at, you don't believe you will have time to properly take care of the dog. Here are three ways to say no:
- No, because my new job is keeping me so busy, I simply don't have the time to take proper care of Fido.
- No, but I bet that teenager down the street would be happy to earn a few bucks taking care of your dog.
- I'll call you later and let you know—I have to check my schedule. (Once you take a good look at your schedule, be honest if you can't take on another responsibility).
- I can take care of the dog on Monday and Wednesday, and I can take the dog for a walk on Saturday if that helps!

Resist the urge to lie when you want to say no. And don't apologize—you have a right to choose what you do and don't have time for. Saying no isn't limited to requests by other people. You may have to say no to yourself too. Taking care of your neighbor's pup may appeal to you—perhaps you're a dog lover living in an apartment with a no- pets policy. But your schedule is already so full that adding another task would put you over the edge. Say no, but offer to take the dog for a long walk some Saturday morning when you have plenty of time. Or say no to something else in your schedule to add in some time for pure joy with the puppy.

Take Action
Connect Without Judgement

Chapter Four - L is for Let Go and Laugh

Many women are incredibly self-judgmental. We criticize ourselves, obsess over even the smallest of flaws, blame ourselves for things that aren't even our fault, and beat ourselves up over the smallest mistakes. If we spoke to other people that way, they would feel awful!

Learning not to judge ourselves is a complicated process that we'll discuss throughout the book. But right now, a very simple and fulfilling way to start tackling all that negative self-judgment is to do an activity I call connecting without judgment.

Here's how it works: For the next week, give something wonderful to everyone you come across. Everyone—your spouse, your kids, your neighbors, the people at work, the bus driver, the guy who cleans your office, the cop directing traffic, the dry cleaner—you get the idea. Give them all a gift: a smile, a positive vibe, a quick silent prayer, a hug, a pat on the back, or a word of encouragement. It doesn't matter what it is as long as it's something positive.

By doing this, you start to accept, in a very small way, that everyone deserves the gift of love without judgment. When you're smiling at someone, you're less likely to judge them. You're nurturing them without judgment. If you can learn how to do this with others, it will become easier for you to do it for yourself.

Mind-Set Purification

Our mind-set has a very powerful effect over our being. One of my favorite writers, philosophers, and teachers, Douglas Pittman, says, in his book Principles for Living on the Edge, "it is estimated that half of the content of our mind, the beliefs, the judgments, and the programs that operate our autopilot are in place by the time we are four years old . . . By the time we are eight years old as much as 80 percent of our belief systems are in place. . . . And as much as 95 percent of our daily actions are generated from this content of our mind, albeit unconsciously."

We all have ingrained thoughts and beliefs about life. Many are simply self-limiting beliefs. These self-limiting beliefs can easily turn into excuses that block us from living out our awesomeness!

It's important to recognize our beliefs and then to test them to determine whether they're true or false. If they're true based on an in- disputable fact and they are working for you in your life, stick with them. But if your beliefs are false or they have become roadblocks, you'll need to let them go and educate yourself so you can replace them with a true, effective set of beliefs. Clinging to a belief system based on failure makes success impossible.

I try to take a no-excuses approach. It doesn't mean we can't have valid reasons not to do something, but we must recognize what they are in order to educate ourselves and make the plan to overcome them. Few things are impossible to the willing heart!

Earlier in the book I shared techniques for being present. One was called "The 3 Lightbulbs".

I often use this light bulb technique to help bring me back to the present moment. First, I visualize clearly and distinctly a specific place where the three lightbulbs would be: one in the trash can (not any trash can, my trash can so the vision is very specific), one in my dining room light fixture, and one in our "odds and ends" cabinet.

Where's the power?

Well, the one in the trash can has no power left. The one in the cabinet has the "promise" of power, but sometimes it's false hope. I mean, haven't you ever screwed in a new lightbulb only to find out it doesn't work? This has happened to me a few times. And the one in the fixture only provides light because of the present moment energy of the bulb actually being properly screwed in to the fixture. On its own, the fixture doesn't provide light nor does the bulb. They need each other, and they need to be plugged in at the moment.

There's a lot in that whole idea of the 3 light bulbs that makes me think. When I'm stuck in the past, I'm giving power to something that has no power. When I'm constantly worrying or hoping or even just thinking about the future, I'm giving power to something that might not even have power. When I'm in the present moment with my energy source (for me, it's God), I have so much power. Without God, on my own, not plugged in, I have little power, if any.

This thought of the 3 light bulbs comforts me. Brings me to the moment. Connects me to my creator. And I can breathe fully, deeply, again. I hold my breath when I am thinking about

Chapter Four - L is for Let Go and Laugh

anything other than now. It might be a subtle hold, but a hold nonetheless, and I absolutely cannot take a full-on breath.

Doug Pitman's book has much about this topic in it - it made me feel like the world was mine to claim. So many stories inspired me, but this one in particular stuck - it was a story about a flea circus.

First off, I didn't realize fleas were actually jumpers. Did you know the average flea can jump about 30 feet??? I always thought that grasshoppers were the jumpers, but fleas actually put grasshoppers to shame.

Second, I forgot about flea circuses. I mean, I heard of them, but I didn't actually know what the term meant, or how they are created. So, I'll explain. A flea circus is usually a traveling amusement where fleas perform. It's a novelty, with miniature carts and such, and it just looks like fleas are participating in a 3-ring circus.

But, it's very hard to train the flea to be in the circus. It takes a lot of time and a big commitment, so we don't see too many flea circuses anymore. Pitman explains that to train a flea, you need to use a series of different size containers, beginning with one the size of a mayonnaise jar.

Basically, you put the flea in the jar, turn the jar upside down, and let the flea do its thing - jump. The flea can jump 30 feet, but the jar is less than a foot tall, so inevitably it hits its head on the top of the jar every time it jumps. The flea realizes it is no fun to hit one's head, so it (eventually) adjusts its jump in fear of getting hurt.

Once the flea has been taught to jump less, the trainer changes to a smaller jar, and repeats this training process until the jar is as small as a baby food jar, and the flea is only jumping about an inch or two.

Now, that flea is ready to perform!

Jar away, jar no longer around the flea, and still, that flea, who was born to jump, no longer jumps 30 feet. It bumped and thumped its head long enough on the top of the jar, that the flea decided life is better if it just doesn't even bother jumping.

Hmmm...

Then Pitman goes on to explain that people actually do the same thing that the flea does. We are born for greatness. We are born to "jump high", but with every negative experience, every demeaning word, we proverbially are placed in a jar, and sadly, we also adjust our jump.

Jar is gone. Experience is over. It's in the past. Like the lightbulb, it's in the trash can, but we still continue to give it power...

Take Action
Inventory Your Excuses and Jars

In your B.A.L.A.N.C.E. Journal, list all the excuses you make. List the experiences in your life that might have created "jars" around your potential. Having awareness around what holds you back and limits you is a beautiful step towards releasing those things. Once you see the words written down, you can test them out, and more often than not, you'll wonder what you were so afraid of!!

B.A.L.A.N.C.E Technique #6
Laughter

Being joyful is the best "cosmetic" I've got in my arsenal of beauty products. And, the price is right.
—Kara Oh

Laughter comes naturally to children. My kiddos are constantly cracking themselves up. They laugh at each other; they laugh at my husband and me; they laugh with their cousins; they laugh at commercials; they laugh and laugh until their bellies hurt. It's adorable, and very contagious.

As adults, sometimes we laugh less frequently, I've come to realize. This is too bad, because laughter, fun, play, and joy are essential ingredients to being in balance. Without these ingredients, we can lose our creativity, our imagination, and our inner child.

Don't say good-bye to that silly little girl inside of you. Reconnect with her—do something completely goofy, laugh out loud, blow some bubbles (without children present), go to a park and swing high on the swings, watch a funny movie, get your girl giggle back even for just a few minutes.

Chapter Four - L is for Let Go and Laugh

Laughter is good for your health. Studies show that thirty minutes of "mirthful laughter" decreases blood levels of the stress hormone cortisol by up to 87 percent!

Prolonged high cortisol levels interfere with the healthy functioning of your thyroid gland as well as your mental performance, bone density, muscle tissue, inflammatory response, and immune system. Excess cortisol can also contribute to blood sugar imbalances, increased body weight, and raised blood pressure.

Laughter boosts immune function, adds oxygen to the blood, stimulates our muscles (that's the best ab workout yet!), and relieves pain.

So take a look at your environment. Does everything about it make you smile? If not, fill your space with joyful images, soothing colors, pictures with meaning, inspiring or fun quotes. Play music, watch movies, tell jokes, pull out old-fashioned games like Twister or Trivial Pursuit, and have a blast at home. Laughing and smiling releases anger and negativity. Simply by having fun, you can live well and show up to the world in all of your awesomeness.

Summing up

In this chapter, we've discussed the tremendous value of undergoing a cleansing process that allows you to let go of the emotional and physical debris that contributes to a life out of balance. Some of the activities I suggested included:

- Do a cabinet and closet cutback that clears your home of clutter and junk. This process helps you commit to a full-scale change that will bring you closer to finding balance.
- Eliminate time vacuums by evaluating and getting rid of some of the things that unnecessarily suck time out of your life.
- Practice saying no so you can give yourself time and energy to focus on living a healthy, balanced life.
- Take a look at your mind-set and purify it of self-limiting beliefs and unhealthy thoughts that knock you off balance.

In chapter 5, I'll help you determine the most important things to add to your daily schedule in order to enrich your life and the lives of others.

Chapter Five
A is for Add In and Appreciate

Be a lamp, a lifeboat, a ladder. Help someone's soul heal. Walk out of your house like a shepherd. - Rumi

When I was a little girl, my family and I watched a movie called Six Weeks. It is about a twelve-year-old girl named Nicole who is dying from leukemia. She wants to do "one Last great thing."

She ends up meeting a politician, and they help each other really live during her final weeks. Nicole skates the ice rink at Rockefeller center, kisses a boy, dances the lead in The Nutcracker, and sightsees in New York city. I loved this movie—it was one of the first times I earned the lesson to live now.

Thinking about it recently made me want to write my own bucket list. But I'm not sure I like the term bucket list. While I love the idea of having one (and the name is pretty catchy), I think a bucket list may never really come to fruition. Most of us feel immortal, and if we think we have all the time in the world to do these things before we "kick the bucket", our goals and dreams may sit in a notebook as we wait for the perfect time to climb our mountains or take our dream vacations. In the movie Six Weeks, Nicole knew how much time she had left. In reality, though, we never know. And there may never be a perfect time to start fulfilling the dreams on our bucket list.

Instead of a bucket list, I opted to write a life list—a list of things I

Chapter Five - A is for Add In and Appreciate

want to do now, not sometime in the distant, hazy future. Writing my life list was such an amazing experience. It made me realize that I had the power to add into my life whatever I wanted, that I could enrich it in such a way that was intentional and purposeful. While some things on my life list were extreme—for example, I'd like to anonymously build a home for someone who lost theirs—I realized there are ways that I could add in service like that without having the funding to actually build the home. I now volunteer with non-profit organizations whose mission is in alignment with my life list goals, to help women and children live with hope and inspiration. But the only way I could find the time and energy to get involved with these organizations was by going through the process of letting go and adding in.

In the previous chapters we've done a brain dump, made assessments, and let go. When you let go, you made time, energy, and space for new things. Now it's time to add in the new things that will enrich your life and the lives of others.

Technique #7
Adding In: To Enrich Your Life and the Lives of Others

As you begin to add things in, consider the differences between a baker and a cook. A baker measures carefully—a teaspoon of this, a tablespoon of that; every ingredient is added in mindfully and intentionally. But cooking is the exact opposite—you toss in a handful of this, a sprinkle of that. Amounts don't really matter. If you love garlic, you throw in a lot; if you don't, you skip it.

So it is in our lives. We need to add in like bakers, measuring carefully. An extra teaspoon of baking powder can throw an entire cake out of balance. In our lives, even a little too much of one thing can cause an imbalance. Like pebbles on a scale, the little things add up fast. Life will naturally sprinkle things in unexpectedly.

Sometimes the sprinkles are fun and surprising, and other times stressful and upsetting. Life is the cook, and we are the bakers. It's up to us to add in with awareness and intention.

How do you know what to add in? One way is to look at the activities you've done so far in this book. Time-use assessments, also from chapter 3, will help you create a schedule that gives you the time you need to meet your obligations, enjoy your life, live healthfully, exercise, take care of yourself, and do the activities you love but thought you didn't have time for. And your excuses inventory from chapter 4 will help you add in new ways of looking at old excuses. Before you start adding in, go back to the core values exercise you did in chapter 2. You can use your core values as a filter to make sure that everything you add in to your life truly reflects your most important values.

I'm not going to tell you exactly what to add in because you need to figure that out for yourself in a way that makes the most sense to you. What you add in will be completely different from what someone else adds in. There are no universal answers, just what's right for you. As you add things to your life, consider these basics to fuel your heart, mind, and body.

- choices that honor your core values
- education
- movement
- healthful, nurturing foods
- time for you
- volunteer opportunities
- a support team

Doing a day design will help you to tap in to your imagination and open your mind to what you can add into your life. Without limitation, obstacles, or boundaries, I want you to grab your B.A.L.A.N.C.E. Journal and just begin writing ideas for how you would spend your day if you had your complete druthers! Resist the urge to write shopping or maxing out my credit cards or sailing away to a deserted island. I understand you may feel like that at times because of how hectic life can be, but this is about truly designing a day that stirs your soul and makes your spirit soar. Just acknowledging these things can begin the process of opening you up to adding them in.

Choosing what to add in is so important because action is what actually creates change. Reading and writing and doing exercises may inspire thought, but our thoughts must be supported by our actions. Otherwise, we can get caught up in a cycle of self-help book after self-help book, without ever really making a shift in thinking or being in the world. I'm sure that's never how the author intends it to be, but that's what can end up happening if we don't take the action in our lives.

I am not a huge fan of self-help books for this reason. That

Chapter Five - A is for Add In and Appreciate

probably sounds weird, since I've written a book that may be considered self-help. Let me explain. I want you to find balance, embrace imperfection, and be who you were born to be. I want you to show up in this world, use your gifts, and enjoy life—you deserve that, I deserve that, we all deserve that, even if we were made to believe differently by another human being or experience. I don't believe that anyone is unworthy. We make mistakes, we learn lessons, we heal, we mess up, and we succeed. I feel we are all students and teachers in our lives in different ways. I believe I was born to communicate. I love to listen to and share stories and to inspire and be inspired by others. What I wish for you is that you take action in your life, nurture yourself, and be confident and strong so you can do that which makes you happy and serves others.

Take Action
What Will You Add-In?

Keep it simple. Begin by writing a list of ten great additions to your daily life and then practicing them one by one. Remember, energy is like an echo: you get back what you put out there. Are you thinking of deprivation or fulfillment? I prefer fulfillment—it's so much more fun than deprivation!

Sometimes when we are aware that we'd like to make a change, we think about all the things we think we've done wrong or we have to stop doing. I know a lot of people who are just plain old beating them- selves up in the name of motivation.

As we discussed in Chapter 4, choosing to let something go can be quite liberating. But if you think you don't have a choice and must do something, you may wind up feeling deprived. If you find that you are discouraged and drowning in a take-away mentality, I suggest flipping your focus to what you want to add in to your life vs. What you want to take away. Once you start adding in healthy, happy, authentic behaviors, your heart, body, and mind will crave more of them, and as a result, more of them will flow naturally into your life! Let's look at some examples:

Take-away mentality: I have to give up sweets.
Add-in mentality: I will eat more veggies.

Take-away mentality: I have to fight less with my partner.
Add-in mentality: I will love and communicate better with my partner.

Take-away mentality: I have to lose this job and do something I really love.
Add-in mentality: I will put passion into whatever I am doing.

Acknowledging, Honoring, and Activating Your Core Values

In chapter 2, you assessed your core values. Now is the time to decide how you will honor and activate those values in your daily life and how those values can be woven into the goals you set for yourself.

I've mentioned that core values act as both an anchor and a compass. Let me explain. I know that life can be busy, stressful, exhausting. I understand that completely, and to be quite honest, I used to believe that my happiness and my balance were dependent on my circumstances—the size of my jeans, the state of my love life, and the title on my business card.

Being aware of it now, I realize how crazy it sounds. But I also know many other women subconsciously feel that way too. Whether it's because of messages from the media or relatives or whoever, women who do not have an anchor can easily get thrown way off balance by circumstances. And without our own internal compass guiding us, we can easily go from self-help book to self-help book looking for the way to happiness. By adding in choices that acknowledge your core values, you strengthen your anchor and fine-tune your compass.

While I have many values, my core values are faith, creativity, inspiration, and family. Just as you have to brush your teeth daily so they don't fall out, you must honor and acknowledge your values daily to keep them strong. So I have daily rituals and visual reminders around each of my core values. I call them my spiritual toothpaste.

For faith, I spend time praying and meditating daily. I read a bit of scripture every morning and evening. I tune in to a faith-based radio station during my drive time. And in my family's home, I have several plaques, pictures, and knickknacks that represent my faith. One of the important things for this core value is to take care of not only my spirit but also my body, because it is a gift from God. So I make sure I nurture my body well.

For creativity, I spend time each day writing, using my

Chapter Five - A is for Add In and Appreciate

imagination (it's kind of easy to nurture imagination when you have children), and doing something creative. Whether it's telling my kids a completely made-up-from-my-mind bed-time story, drawing, making a gift basket for our family business, or making picture collages, each day I do something to honor my value of creativity. On the days I don't honor my creativity, I feel fenced in.

I value creativity with food too. I can't just chomp on celery all day, and the thought of plain anything bores me. I crave flavor! I am a creative foodie crunched for time, so I buy all different kinds of spices, herbs, and pure extracts. With these tools, it's easy to create simple, unique foods. Forget about thirty-minute meals—I specialize in thirty-second meals! Some days I blend up wheat germ, almond milk pure coconut extract, frozen blueberries, and a pinch of fine shredded coconut, and I feel like I am on a tropical island. Other days, my taste buds take me to a cozy winter cabin so I add cinnamon, nutmeg, pure vanilla extract, and diced warm apples to plain oatmeal. I mash avocado with garlic and lime juice for a burst of flavor that's yummy on just about anything or even simply by the spoon. You can be creative without spending hours on complicated recipes.

For inspiration, I like to both inspire and be inspired. In order to acknowledge this value, I have a blog called Inspired Girl. I share my personal life lessons and stories in hopes of inspiring my readers, and I interview other inspiring women who share their stories. I also teach classes that inspire and take classes to be inspired. I receive a daily dose of inspiration in my inbox, and I send inspirational messages to my e-mail list. It's a circle of inspiration!

For family, all my decisions are made with the greater good of my family in the front of my mind. Spending time with my family is incredibly important for me because time and presence are the most precious gifts we can give the people we love. I realize my children may not remember the "stuff" they once had, but they will remember us spending time in the kitchen together, out in the yard climbing trees, or walking on the beach collecting shells. Our photo albums are filled with experiences, not things.

There have been times when I could have worked longer hours to see more clients and earn more income, but I chose not to so I could be home with my family. There are also times when I am required to travel for work, and I know by doing so I am able to provide for my family. On a daily basis, I make sure I spend quality time with my children, speak on the phone with my parents, and drink coffee on the porch with my husband. I consciously value my family, and my decisions are centered on them. It really is all about defining your own meaning and method for balance.

I also know that being a healthy, happy, balanced mom is so important for my family, so I must spend time taking care of me too. When I am going for a walk, doing yoga, or eating fresh, delicious food, I am honoring my Family value.

Take action
Let Your Core Values Guide You

Write down each of your core values, and then describe how you can honor and recognize them on a daily basis. Make sure you also think about your life vision and goals, and weave the core values into them as well. If you aren't honoring your values daily (that is, you lack spiritual toothpaste) figure out ways to do just that so your values are strong, your anchor is sturdy, and your compass is pointed in the right direction. And remember, when you let your core values guide you, you won't be as attached to outcomes. You'll feel so good, you'll enjoy the process!

Add In Education

Educating yourself may sound boring. But it is so important. The more we truly understand something, the easier it is to implement in our lives. And once we begin understanding, learning becomes more and more invigorating. For example, I used to think nothing of drinking orange juice—who has time to peel and eat an actual orange? Besides the juice has vitamin c so it's really no different, right? Wrong!

When I learned that the digestion process was completely different when you eat an orange versus drinking the juice, it really made me stop and think. The white rind on the orange provides fiber that pre- pares your body for the sugar in the fruit of the orange. When you bite into the rind, the fiber sends a signal to your body. It aids the digestion of the fruit—something that doesn't happen when you're drinking a carton of processed orange juice.

Because I was prediabetic, I choose to watch my sugar intake carefully. After learning that the full fruit is near perfect in form, from

Chapter Five - A is for Add In and Appreciate

skin to pulp, I made time to eat oranges instead of just drinking juice. If you're reaching for orange juice instead of soda, it's a healthier option for sure. But the real benefits from fruit often are found in skin and pulp, which is generally absent in juice (even 100 percent fruit juice). My point is this: educate yourself on your options, and then make informed decisions that are best for you.

I encourage you to empower yourself with education. If you were sitting in your living room and the lights went out, what would you do? Probably check the switch and replace the bulb. If those things didn't work, you might check the circuit breaker and, if necessary, call in an electrician. You wouldn't simply sit in the dark or light a candle as a temporary fix. But we often sit in the dark when it comes to our lives. Turn on the light! Learn as much as you can about your body, your spirit, and your mind to understand the way each functions best.

Add In Miracles

Alright, who doesn't want a miracle of some sort to show up in her life? Think about Monday mornings - a time when people all around the world choose to begin again. A new day. A new week - ah yes, the feeling of renewal happens naturally when Monday rolls around...

But, renewal actually happens every day - moment to moment, second to second in our lives. Everything from our cells to our skin to our thoughts is in a constant state of change. I once heard Marianne Williamson describe a "miracle" as a shift in thinking that causes a shift in our experiences.

Wow. Imagine, in any moment, on any given day of the week, a simple shift in thought could create a miracle in your life?

The actions we take are directly related to the thoughts we have. The thoughts we have can be rooted in truth or false truth. When our thoughts are rooted in truth, it opens us up for the miracle to occur.

So is the miracle simply thought or thought + action? This goes back to your truth. My truth is seek and we shall find - whatever we are seeking, we shall find it, when we seek with all of our hearts.

According to the dictionary, seek is an action word meaning "to try" or "endeavor". I believe that when thoughts and actions are in alignment, that allows God the space to come do His work.

However, sometimes the actions are not what directly creates the miracle, if that were the case, where would God fit in? God does the behind the scenes work that we simply cannot explain.

I recently listened to Pastor Rick Warren discuss the correlation between thought and action on Oprah's Lifeclass. This is something I've studied for over almost twenty years, and have experienced (in both positive and no-so-positive ways) in my own life. When we witness both of these positive or not-so-positive effects, it can lead to incredible opportunities for growth, blessings, and lessons.

So, when you know you want something different in your life, why can it be so difficult sometimes to do something different in order to facilitate the change(s) you want?

Simply put., I will describe the path to action like this -

Beliefs create thoughts. Sometimes we consciously choose beliefs, but many times limiting beliefs are created out of false truths dictated by experiences or external factors (including other people).

What is truth? If you are believing false truth, that creates a ripple effect in your life. A false truth is anything you do not declare as truth. The thing is, we can choose what is truth and what is false truth.

For me, I believe each of us is capable of more than we know because my truth is "With God, all things are possible." (Matthew 19:26). Anything that counters that statement is a false truth.

Step 1: Know your truth, and do not let false truths become your beliefs. False truths usually have no real 'roots', they have little to know substance, can often be fear-based, and they can even sometimes just be unintentional ignorant words from another human being that end up becoming your (false) truth. Root or anchor your truth in something deep.

What is your truth? What do you believe?

Thoughts create feelings. If we think something, that thought is often translated into a feeling. The feeling creates an energy or

Chapter Five - A is for Add In and Appreciate

mood that takes over our entire presence. When we feel something, everyone around us knows it, and feels it, too.

Step 2: Know how you feel, and create a level of awareness around the gaps between how you want to feel versus how you actually feel. Do you like how you're feeling? Is your spark for life fully lit? Do you feel positive about the possibilities or are you feeling stuck in status quo?

If we want to feel differently, we have to think and believe differently. See Step 1 and repeat until you feel like the magnificent person you were born to be :)

How do you feel?

Feelings create our words. So, we believe something to be truth, we think about it a lot, it makes us feel a certain way, and all of the sudden, we are speaking that (sometimes false) truth to ourselves and to others. Words give our thoughts more power, which can be used to our benefit or to hold us back from our true potential.

Step 3: Speak words that support your truth. Are your words powerful, kind, loving, positive, a mirror of who you are at the core, reflecting what you want deep down on the inside OR are your words negative, weak, hurtful, solely a reflection of what "is" or what no longer serves you or the greater good?

What are your words saying?

Our words create our actions. Yes, when you believe it, think it, feel it, say it, you take action on it!! If you don't like the actions you are taking, and know you want to take different actions, you have to fuel your beliefs with 'heart fuel' that lights you up, and fuel your thoughts with 'mind fuel' that renews you, that restores you, that lifts you up!!

Step 4: Take actions that align with the amazing person you are. If you know you want something, stand firm in your truth, feel incredible, speak greatness towards yourself and others, and take action that will support and strengthen your life mission.

Who were you born to be?

One Last Thing! I know this is written in "steps", but it can also be seen as a "circle" - the awesome thing about our connectedness in humanity, is that sometimes, others can lift us up in our truth, even when we don't fully believe it or feel it. But, by taking action that aligns with it, we can strengthen our own beliefs, and change our thoughts, feelings, words, actions...

Add In Foods That You Love, Nurture You, & Fill You Up

In case you haven't already noticed, I'll just say it: I love food! I am a foodie through and through, and I definitely do not believe that we should deprive ourselves of enjoying food. As I mentioned, I love food so darn much, I married a chef. It was a prerequisite for the guys I dated: if they didn't love food or know how to cook, they were out. I am serious about loving and enjoying food.

To begin adding in your favorite foods, do a brain dump and list them all in your B.A.L.A.N.C.E Journal. Include every last chip, candy bar, and rich sauce. Get it all on paper. If you love pizza, write it down. Chicken Francais, Chinese fried rice, cheesecake, french toast, waffles with syrup, eggplant Parmesan, barbecue potato chips, chocolate chip cookies—acknowledge what you love. Then you can begin to figure out ways to make a healthy and delicious version of the same flavors and textures.

For example, if you love pizza, it doesn't make sense to decide that you'll never eat it again just because it's high in calories and fat. That is unrealistic, and it's also not necessary. You can figure out ways to make pizza as healthy as possible so you can eat it every week and enjoy it. One of my clients chooses flatbread pizza because it is much lower in carbohydrates and calories than doughy pizza. Another pulls off half the cheese. Another has her favorite loaded pizza but eats only one slice instead of her usual three or four.

I believe that people love the flavors and textures of their favorite foods, not necessarily the food itself. I used to say I loved peanut butter cups. But I realized I actually loved the combination of chocolate and peanut butter together in a compact bite. So when I'm craving a peanut butter cup, I choose instead to have a dark chocolate square with a bit of natural peanut butter. It satisfies my desire for peanut butter and chocolate in a much healthier way.

One of my absolute favorite flavors is coconut. During a trip to the Turks and Caicos islands a few years back, I discovered that I adore coconut-crusted chicken and fish. I had to figure out a way to make coconut-crusted food a staple, but in a healthy way. So after a little trial and much error, I came up with a Caribbean-inspired, delicious, healthy, and super-simple meal. Instead of dipping the chicken in whole eggs, I combine two egg whites with one whole egg and add a splash of pure coconut extract. This way, I get an extra flavor of the coconut. For the crust, I mix Panko bread crumbs with finely shredded coconut. A finer shred of coconut allows me to use less and eliminate about 40 percent of the calories and fat. I also bake it in the oven instead of frying. It is coconut-crusted deliciousness!

Next take a look at your food assessment Worksheet in chapter 3. What's missing from your usual daily diet? Some of my clients realize they eat zero vegetables (iceberg lettuce on a Big Mac doesn't count). They eat no dark, leafy greens or colorful yellow, orange, or red fruits and vegetables, all of which are bursting with cancer-fighting antioxidants and loads of other great nutrients. I understand, I was one of those people too.

Add in healthy, nutritious, filling foods—vegetables, fruits, legumes, whole grains. Often when you add in these foods, the less healthy foods drop out of your diet naturally because you're too full to eat them!

You may also notice from your Food Assessment Worksheet that you aren't eating satiating foods, that the calories seem empty and don't really fill you up. If so, try adding in satiating whole grains. For breakfast, choose oatmeal with diced peaches or scrambled eggs on whole-grain toast. Enjoy a bowl of carrot and cashew soup between lunch and dinner. Fish—especially thick, white fish—is high on the satiety index, so cut it into cubes, toss it on the grill with some vegetables, and serve over brown rice for a filling meal.

Add In Fuel for Your Senses for the 3 Critical Fuel Sources

Remember in Chapter One I shared the 3 Critical Fuel Sources - Heart, Mind, and Physical Body? Well, we are subliminally fueling ourselves all of the time through our senses. Let me explain.

One of my favorite things in the whole world is cozy, lounge around the house foot gear. I love love love comfy socks. And, all of my slippers are lined with soft material. I have a theory - happy feet = happy soul.

This theory is based on my personal experience with awfully

uncomfortable shoes.

Yes, anyone who knew me years ago, knew I had a thing for shoes. While they were lovely to look at, and at that time in my life I didn't feel or notice the discomfort they caused, I am simply not the same person any longer. Yep, my kiddos can't even imagine me wearing a pair of heels - I had to show them pictures as proof!!

The Turning Point: About six years ago I went to the Women Entrepreneurs Rock the World conference in NYC. I was so excited to go to see women I hadn't seen in a while and meet new, amazing women! The mistake I made - I wore heels. And I didn't bring any alternatives. By the end of the day, while my heart was so excited, my body began to rebel. I had to sit, I couldn't connect the same way, I was in massive pain...I learned my lesson, wear comfy shoes, or ALWAYS bring comfy shoe #2 "waiting in the wings".

Soft socks and fuzzy slippers not only feel good on our feet, but the "feel good" feeling comes through in our facial expressions, our tone of voice, our overall state-of-being. We connect with humanity so much better when we are comfortable inside and out.

All this through a pair of comfy shoes? YES!! But it's not just comfortable shoes, we are brilliantly designed human beings. And there is healing power through our senses, (particular to the shoe story) - the power of 'touch' through our somatosensory system.

"The somatosensory system (somatosensory nervous system or SNS) is a complex system of nerve cells that responds to changes to the surface or internal state of the body."

The research is clear - there are over 100 studies on how touch can lift our mood, provide comfort, peace of mind, solace, even boost the immune system...so today, try incorporating something soothing by way of this sense.

Healing Hands
We don't always have time or money to have a massage, although it is very powerful for relieving stress. If you have a partner, make sure to hold hands and connect with him/her. Find your favorite furry four-legged friend and pet away! Flying solo? You can give yourself a temple massage, adding in an aromatic oil will amp it up a notch. For a simple soother, try warming a wet towel and wrapping it around your hands or neck.

Chapter Five - A is for Add In and Appreciate

The Blankie Effect
Remember "woobies" work for a reason! Touch can happen in many forms, it doesn't have to be physical contact. Ever notice how a child clings to his/her teddy bears or favorite blankets, especially when they are tired or teary eyed? Cuddle up to a velvet pillow, or put your blanket in the dryer for a few minutes to warm it up, and wrap it around you while watching TV. Keep your sheets and bedding soft, too.

Comfy from Head to Toe
Wearing clothing that feels good - from fleece pajamas to a satin shirt- can work wonders on your mood. And don't forget your feet as I mentioned! Use gel inserts for your heels, or even keep fuzzy, soft-lined slippers under your desk or around the house. Aching feet cause a lot of stress throughout our bodies. Remember, physical stress can lead to mental stress and vice versa.

FUEL ALL OF YOUR SENSES

While the sense of touch has such a powerful impact on our being, so do all of the senses. What we taste, smell, see, hear, touch all creates fuel for our bodies, minds, and hearts. Often, we unconsciously are being fed fuel that isn't in alignment with what our core being values, but the fuel is so strong it affects our mood, our attitude, our actions. Let me give you an example!

A few years back one of my clients was upset over the relationship she had with her husband. She said when they first got married, they were very much in love. But, lately (and 15 years later with 2 kids, far more hectic work schedules, and much higher bills), they were arguing or annoyed with each other daily. She said she'd walk in the door from work and within minutes they were on edge with one another.

When I asked her what they would fight about, she basically said everything. Sometimes it was an all out argument, other times it was just a cold shoulder, and other times they were just slamming doors with no words exchanged. She said she didn't like how she behaved towards him, and she didn't know what was making her cold.

She began to talk about things that he did that upset her, but as she was complaining about how he doesn't ever know what he wants for dinner or that he leaves the cabinet doors open and dishes in the sink, she realized most of what was upsetting her was trivial. So why would it escalate so much?

Curious myself, I asked her a bit more about her commute home. Since the common thread with their tension was it began as soon as she walked in the door from work, I wondered if her drive time had anything to do with her demeanor.

She said her commute was fine, she drove about 25 - 30 minutes, and she listened to talk radio because she loved listening to people debate. And, she loved being informed about current events.

So I asked her to try something different the next day. I suggested finding a radio station or putting music on a CD (yes I said it was a few years ago!!) that was from the time that they were dating. Upbeat songs, love songs, just a mix of some of their favorites.

Now, you may think such a minor change wouldn't really make a difference. My client thought so, too. She didn't really see the point, she thought they were beyond music. But, the thing is, music creates a feeling, and that feeling is transferred as energy through our facial expressions, our body language, even our words. My thought was, perhaps talk radio, as much as she loved it, amped her up too much on the way home, and she walked in a little jumpy. Even if she didn't say a word, her husband could be misinterpreting her energy and reacting to it negatively.

Also, I had no idea what her husband's commute was like or what was happening during his day. He could have many stressors also, and the two combined could be creating this marital disconnect. Since we can only control our own actions / reactions / fuel sources, I was focusing on my client. But I had a sneaking suspicion there was more to it on his end as well.

Once my client opened up to changing the radio station, she said she almost immediately felt better. She was flooded with happy memories, and it showed. Her husband noticed the change, and the two of them committed to communicating better and being more mindful of their energy, not bringing 'home' the stress of the day.

Here are some ways you can also fuel yourself well through your senses:

Bring Back the Ocean Breeze

Chapter Five - A is for Add In and Appreciate

Make your space visually appealing, whether it be your car, home, or office. Try hanging a picture of a place that calms you or reminds you of a happy time and place. Perhaps your vacation was a dream, or your baby girl's smile melts your heart. Make sure you have *intentional* visual reminders around you of all that brings a smile to your face! You can even paint your walls a color that makes you feel content and calm. If you have old wallpaper up that you can't stand, take it down- a coat of paint goes a long way to creating a peaceful space.

Listen Up

With ipods, itunes and built-in computer speakers, it's simple to have calming sounds playing softly at your desk, in your car, or in your home. And if you want to listen to music, choose tunes that make you happy. Sound can also be impacted by the shows we watch, the conversations we partake in or overhear, the background sounds we hear. I've had clients literally feel like they don't measure up because their homes weren't decorated like the dream homes they saw on HGTV.

Scent-Sational Relief

Ok, so we all know about aromatherapy. Don't underestimate the value of dabbing a little oil on your wrists, keeping beautiful smelling candles lit, wearing your favorite perfume. Vanilla, ginger, lavender, lemon, chamomile, sandalwood, ylang ylang, and bergamot are all proven to have anti-stress effects. Find the scents that calm you down and use them in your environment.

Taste the Way to Calm

Don't misinterpret this one-this does not mean stress eating. There are certain flavors, textures, and temperatures of food/beverage that have proven calming effects. There is a huge correlation to stress and digestion, affecting the way we feel in general. Herbal teas and warm milk can relax you. Also, eating at a relaxed pace in regular intervals is important-don't go hours on end without eating and then shovel in something quick. Caffeine and simple sugar stimulate stress, so if you reach for a candy bar and an energy drink, stop yourself. You'll feel worse afterward!

You might not even realize it, but all the ways we use our senses can be uplifting and healing or depressing and debilitating - it's transformative when we choose wisely. I'm certain you are doing lots already that fuels your senses well. Maybe you have a favorite song you turn to (sound), or a favorite candle you light (smell), or your bedroom is painted your favorite calming hue (sight), or you sip on your favorite tea (taste), or schedule a nice spa pedicure (touch)...you get my drift!!

Take Action
Choose Uplifting Sensory Activities
How can you incorporate the healing power of our senses into your life? Begin noticing the ways you already are using your senses. Grab your B.A.L.A.N.C.E Journal and brain dump. On the next page, write with each sense as the header, and write things that lift you up that you can incorporate into your life for each.

Add in Passion, Zest, and Zeal for Life

If you haven't already noticed, I am taking a stand against women feeling less than because of their size, hair color, financial situation, or relationship status. I think a woman who just plain old lives in her authenticity is the most beautiful woman in the world.

I know what it's like to feel less than—I've been there and could probably write an entire book about that topic. But it would be B-O-R-I-N-G! The bottom line is that you don't need to look a certain way, wear a certain label, hold a certain job title, or have a certain someone in order to be absolutely beautiful from the inside out. You don't even need to know your purpose.

There is one way to instantly glow, and that is to live by your values, and put passion into everything you do. Then your purpose will unfold naturally, and you won't have to work like a bull to figure it out. People will come into your life because your passion and love for life will bring them to you. You will take care of yourself because you love yourself and we nurture what we love.

I am inspired by many women, all of whom share this in common: they are kind, their unique energy radiates from within, they are compassionate and they serve the world with their gifts. These are the women who rock in my book. Put love into everything you do, say, and see. Judge nothing, not even yourself. Look at the world through a passionate lens!

Chapter Five - A is for Add In and Appreciate

Here are three simple steps to adding in passion, zest, and zeal for life:

1. Look within. You don't have to leave happiness up to chance— you have the power to be your best self every single day. In your B.A.L.A.N.C.E. Journal, answer these simple questions to identify how you can be your best self:

    When are you smiling and laughing the most? When do you feel most 'alive'? Describe exactly what you are doing, where you are, who you are with.

2. Take advantage of the little you moments. Little you moments are the opportunities you have throughout your day to pamper yourself in small but meaningful ways. They include the way your space is designed, the music you listen to in the car, the lotions and face wash you use, the scent of your shampoo, the weekly at-home spa treatments you give yourself. Little you moments are the best, and they fit seamlessly into your life! By taking advantage of little you moments, you are practicing self-care at a proactive, preventive level.

    Self-care on a preventive level helps keep you feeling balanced even when life is hectic, stressful, and exhausting. Then when a big stressor comes along, you're better prepared for it.

3. Have regular date nights. Every girl needs a date night every now and then. It doesn't have to be romantic—it just needs to get you away from the stresses of everyday life and make you smile. You can date your spouse, your friends, your sister, your entire family, or even yourself. Do whatever is fun—go out or stay in. Go to a restaurant with pals. Or stay home, run a bath, light a candle, pour your favorite drink, and read a book. If you and the girls haven't gone clubbing in decades, hit the club and dance it up. If you and your husband crave a night out but don't have much time or money to spare, make a mini-date—converse over coffee at a dimly lit café, grab a glass of wine and listen to music, share an appetizer at your favorite restaurant. It will be quick, but it's just enough time to connect.

    Date nights should happen regularly and be built right in

to your schedule. If weekly date nights are impossible, make them biweekly or once a month. The important relationships in our lives should never suffer because of lack of time, so make it a point to get together as often as realistically possible. Date nights can be spontaneous or planned. The only rule is that they have to be fun. Here are some examples:

- Create a carpet picnic in the living room and surprise someone special. Go all out and include a picnic basket, flowers, wine, and dessert.
- View the night sky from a mountain, hill, or beach. Lie on the ground and look at the moon. Bring a map of the constellations on a clear night and search away.
- Get lost! Fill up your gas tank, turn on the tunes, and take a mini road trip to nowhere. Explore a town you are unfamiliar with and find a spot to eat, walk, and learn about the town's history from some locals.
- Support talent in your town. Many local bars, restaurants, bookstores, galleries, and libraries invite artists, musicians, or writers to share their talent. Check out your newspaper or go online to find something unique happening in your own backyard.
- Dress to the nines for no reason! You may have a gown sitting in your closet that you've only worn once. I'm sure your friends may too!
- Plan a girls' night out or take your mate on a date. You don't have to go for fancy food—you can walk around town window shopping, go to a boardwalk, or just hit a local coffee shop.
- Take a cooking class or hire a chef (or culinary school apprentice) to come to your home and give a private cooking lesson. It sounds extravagant, but you may be able to find student chefs willing to do this just for the experience of cooking and teaching.

Take Action
Brainstorm Little You Moments

Do a brain dump that lists ways to turn ordinary moments into little you moments. For example:
- Create a spa in the shower with special scented soap and a fluffy white washcloth.

- Wear comfy slippers around the house.
- Use high thread count sheets.
- Choose a meaningful mug for sipping morning tea or coffee.
- Wake up fifteen minutes early and spend time reading, meditating, stretching, or just being before the day's chaos begins.
- Make a mixed CD or special iPod playlist with your favorite tunes to listen to while driving or working out.
- Use a special oil treatment for your hair and let it soak in while you do laundry or other household duties.
- Rub essential oils into your temples.
- Lube your legs with your favorite lotion.
- Do something completely silly while cleaning the house.
- Eat your lunch on a blanket in the grass.
- Take a warm milk bath.

Add In Connecting to Combat Stress

In our lightning-paced, media-laced, rat-raced world, we are bombarded by every kind of stress conceivable.

While everyone handles stress differently, I've noticed that to live with these stressors, some people may choose to use a cynical or dismissive posture like a shield to deflect all that comes in their path. I believe that coldness and anger are really just hurts or fears that have hardened. And, when we're hard like that, nothing sticks. So, many become more connected to their iPhones than the people in the world around them. In time, it makes this "disconnected" state-of-being the norm, and that actually makes stress more acute.

With natural disasters, incredible tragedies, financial crises, and so on, it is difficult to turn your head down to your electronic device, and not realize that something needs to give, right? .This is the first generation of children predicted to not outlive their parents due to stress-related issues, and the number of people who reported stress-related problems in the past few years has gone up immensely.

Ok, yes, stress is real, life is imperfect. Earlier in this chapter, I equate this to the difference between the baker and the cook. Anyone who likes to cook knows that when you're cooking, you can sprinkle in a little of this and add a dash of that without the real need to "measure" anything out. Sometimes the dish tastes delicious, and other times, well let's just say WAY TOO MUCH

GARLIC!! Life is like the cook - it sprinkles stuff in unexpectedly that turns out to be amazing, and sometimes, it gives us something that is just awful.

But, in baking, there is little room to sprinkle or dash anything - you have to measure things out carefully or you end up with a big flop completely inedible!! Let life be the "cook", we are the bakers. And, to be like "bakers' in our lives, everything we do is a choice, and we choose to add things in to our lives with purpose and intention.

So, while "stress" is a part of life, we can choose to do things to combat the negative effects of stress, so we can stay connected to the world around us, our purpose, and get back to basics - humanity...

If we choose to make a difference, touch lives, connect with our goodness and share our strengths the cynicism melts away. These can be little gestures, or bold, committed actions. If you take tens of millions of them every day and turn them loose on the world, our lives, ALL of our lives, will be noticeably better...

Here are 3 examples of things we can do to melt the cynicism and stress away, touch lives, connect with our each other, and make our own lives better in the process:

Share your gifts - Focus on what you CAN do, what your GIFTS are, and serve others from the heart...when we help others, we heal ourselves. If you love to paint, offer to paint a friend's home or office or go to your local shelter and offer to paint there! If you love to scrapbook, offer to scrapbook your friend's photos or make a scrapbook collage for your child's school.

Share in Your Community - Get involved in your neighborhood by using your talents to organize an event - if you're a musician, create a Neighborhood Jam Night, if you love to cook, try a Town Tasting where home cooks can share their tastiest creations, if you love sports, set up an Annual Football on the Square event! You get my drift.

Volunteer with a Nonprofit- Share your gifts with a nonprofit organization and offer to do something for them that lights you up. If you're a knitter, offer to knit blankets for children. If you're an artist, paint a mural or create a tile wall in a shelter or hospital. If you're a baker, make homemade cookies to take to community

Chapter Five - A is for Add In and Appreciate

center...you get my drift.

Connect with Children- Either in your local school, shelters, places of worship, there are children everywhere we can serve with our time and talent. Teach a child your favorite skill or hobby, and your spirit will soar!

Be a Supporter - Hold others up in your highest regard. Support somebody's dreams or aspirations. If you are having a hard time being a supporter, surround yourself with people who hold you in their highest regard, and naturally you will begin to do the same for others. True supporters know each other's strengths, abilities, and flaws, and believe in each other no matter what! Find supporters at your local church, community service organization, friendship circles, or faith-based networking groups and online communities.

Be a Teacher and Be Open to Learning from Great Teachers- Teaching gives us a sense of purpose and value that naturally relieves stress because we are connecting with others on something we are truly passionate about! And, our lives are always teaching others just by our actions. There are lots of ways you can 'teach' without necessarily being a school teacher.

Live and Take Action - What do you want to teach? What would you like to learn? Take action on those things!! Our lives are always teaching others just by the actions we take. Sure, I can write about kindness and teach a class about kindness, but if I ignore the man holding the door for me to walk into the classroom, I am actually teaching coldness. Let your life be your lesson and your classroom, where you constantly learn and teach.

Join a Group, Network, or Organization - Share yourself, your life lessons, your mistakes, your successes with a group or network. Share your knowledge and connect with others who have something to share with you as well. You can even offer to teach a class on a skill, passion, or hobby that would enrich the group and give you an opportunity to help others!

Be a Mentor - I am so grateful to the many mentors I've met in my lifetime - some knew they were mentoring me, while others just ended up being a great mentor by their actions and words. So, if an opportunity arises for me to mentor someone on something I've learned, I share what I can with them. If a person has the courage to ask me to be a mentor, I am eager to help.

I am also careful to remember that teachers come in many forms, not just older, wiser people. Nature has been a great teacher to me – learning from birds that while soaring looks simple, it takes a lot of work, even pain, to learn how to fly, and often that bird was kicked out of its nest by its mother. My children, my precious gifts from God, have been my greatest teachers. They remind me every day of our essence, who we are each born to be. And what do they love the most? Sharing, listening, connecting, being present, looking at the moon and stars in the sky, telling me a silly story, laughing, giggling, dancing, living...

Add In a Support System: Enlist the Troops and Build a Team

My husband was an athlete in high school. He played football, and he often tells me stories about the good old days with the guys. He had an incredible coach and assistant coach as well as a whole team of people who worked together with common goals in mind: to win, to play the sport well, and to learn something from every game.

As in sports, we are all more likely to succeed if we have a team of supportive people working with us to achieve a common goal.

Many women have support teams for finances, accounting, legal issues, events such as weddings, and even for their hair and nails. But for some reason, sadly, many women choose to go through life alone or without deep supportive relationships.

Support is one of the best predictors of success, especially when it comes to making changes. There are two basic types of support we need when making a life change: support of knowledge (information, examples, education, action) and support of people (family, friends, groups, coaches, health care providers).

Support of knowledge: You're reading this book, so you're already educating yourself and are in the process of self-discovery. I encourage all my clients to always continue acquiring knowledge. Read books, take courses, ask questions, and listen to other people's stories. Constant learning is one of the best ways to stay connected with your goals.

Most wellness professionals will tell you the reason they are so committed to living well and teaching others how to do so is the knowledge they have about the subject. Just knowing that everyday choices like how much we move or what we eat can affect our

Chapter Five - A is for Add In and Appreciate

entire being (from mood to energy levels to state of health confidence to relationships), it's near impossible to choose anything but whole options. This knowledge not only comes from continual coursework and reading, but also from working with people who have a similar mission to be in balance. This is one of the reasons I believe that when we teach what we once most needed to learn, it reinforces our education and keeps us connected to our personal goals, so we can be who we were born to be.

Support of people: I know firsthand how important it is to have the support of people. My family and friends are an integral support team in my life. I also have a professional support team of colleagues, mentors, and networking groups. Each of my supporters serves a somewhat different role in my life. Of course, I have my husband and our parents, who are supportive no matter what. I call my friend Jessica when I need a voice of reason. My sister-in-law, Danielle, listens, questions, and helps come up with solutions; and there's Jess, who's practically like a younger sister! She listens without judgment—she loves me, flaws and all. My dear friend Marta is also a supporter, or Vanessa, who has a strong anchor in faith, and they always say just the right words. For encouragement and pure love, my friend Jessica and I co-founded a group called "S.O.A.R", and the women in our community are there to cheer each other on or lift each other up or just allow us each to be our unique selves. For business issues, I turn to my Uncle Paul, my entrepreneurial friends, or online community. Not only in business issues but also in helping work through challenges or simply savoring our success together—their support is incredible. When I set a goal, I usually find a mentor or coach to support me through the process.

Knowing who to go to for what type of support I need eliminates a whole bunch of time I would spend calling everyone I know and rambling.

Before I make a phone call or enlist a supporter, I take a beat just to listen to my heart. Sometimes the need to reach out to someone goes away and I find peace within. I believe God is always there to listen and support us. He also sends divinely appointed angels that come at just the right moment, saying just the right thing. Of course, there are other times, when I reach out to the person in my mental rolodex who can give me the type of support I need. I try to be the same type of support for the people in my life, the strangers I interact with - we can't go this journey alone. We all need one another.

Support can come from family, friends, coworkers, an online group, a group, a class, a community, or a personal coach, just to name a few. Believe it or not, I found a great supporter just by frequenting the same Dunkin' Donuts (for coffee, of course) daily.

We can read books, take courses, and fill out worksheets, but we must complement this knowledge with what we learn from the actions and experiences of others—not from their preaching, but from their stories, choices, and the example of how they live.

Parents are a great example of this. A mother may tell her child to be kind to others. But this lesson is far more meaningful when a child observes her mother's kindness in action. We are in a constant state of teaching and learning just by being. If you want to teach people joy, you must be joyful—and by being joyful, you are learning joy. If you want to teach people strength, you must be strong, and then you are learning strength.

Supporters are people who hold you in their highest regard. They see you as your best self and love you even when you are your worst. If a friend or relative is constantly focusing on your perceived negative qualities and never shining a light on your strengths, this person may not be your first choice as a supporter.

Take Action
Form Your Team

In your B.A.L.A.N.C.E. Journal, make a list of people in your life who lift you up. This could include your spouse, parents, family, friends, or any combination of them. Then expand your view to a pastor at church or a rabbi at temple, a neighbor who always says hello, or a dear co-worker. It could be someone you chat with online, a former teacher, or someone you admire from afar. Once you identify your supporters and mentors, you may want to formalize the relationship and ask them to be part of your support team.

The keys with enlisting the support of people is to first clarify your definition of support and then to take the leap and ask people to become your supporters.

I've worked with many women who say they are surrounded by unsupportive people. I understand. But I believe there are many people who genuinely want to see you succeed at what you set out

Chapter Five - A is for Add In and Appreciate

to do. They just may not know how to do that. We all have different definitions of support, and we certainly can't expect people to know ours unless we articulate it to them. Communication and clarity are crucial. Once you set up support guidelines, you may be shocked at just how supportive the people in your life can be.

Here are some tips to keep in mind while you form your support team:

Be clear about what you're asking for. If you don't communicate the fact that you are looking for support, friends and family may choose to stay silent. For example, if you tell your husband you are trying to achieve a goal, he may think you don't want to hear anything from him, so he will keep his mouth shut! People sometimes don't want to overstep, so make sure whoever you are putting on your support team knows (and accepts) that they are enlisted.

Be clear about what kind of support you need. How do you feel best supported? For example, you may tell your friend that you want to release some weight and take control of your health. Once she has agreed to support you, she may think the best way to do this is to point out when you're eating something she thinks you shouldn't. This won't help if you hate being monitored by food police. So be clear and communicative about your goals and what your expectation or need for sup- port is. Support can be physical: you may find it helpful to have a supporter go food shopping or walking with you. Support can also be emotional: you may find it beneficial to have someone you can

Discuss your challenges and successes with. Support can also be encouragement: ideally, your supporters will inspire and encourage you with kind words, praise, and observations. For example, you may want your supporters to notice little things you are doing differently and compliment you on the changes you've made.

Understand that not everyone can be an effective supporter for you. Often people try to be supportive, but even when you clearly explain your goals, they can't give you what you need. That's okay. People who love you can't necessarily support you in the way you want or need. Be grateful, acknowledge their efforts, and recognize that you may need to enlist a different supporter.

I worked with a woman whose mother tried so hard to support her. No matter how many times she told her mother she didn't want her to focus on the calories she ate or the number on the scale, her mother couldn't help herself. One day it turned into a huge argument. My client felt awful. Her mother felt hurt. I advised my client to recognize her mother's efforts but not to expect her mother to change her own ingrained dieter's mentality. Then my client chose to enlist support from her cousin, even though they hadn't talked in a while. Her cousin was happy to hear from her and was quite willing to take over as her chief supporter. My client still spoke with her mother regularly, and because she was receiving the support she needed elsewhere, she could let go of being continually frustrated by unmet expectations and begin to appreciate her mother for who she was.

Show gratitude to your supporters. Thank them for their support, encourage them in their endeavors, and offer to be a member of their support team in return.

One Last Thing!

This might not be something to "add in" but it is important and will enrich your life and the lives of other. There are two small shifts that can catapult us from dreaming about doing something to being the person we were born to be.

Shift #1: See yourself as you want to be—now. We live up to the expectations and the image we hold for ourselves. We must see and believe that we are complete, whole, capable, resourceful individuals. If you have an intention, phrase it in the present tense. Replace passive, wishful phrases ("I wish I could succeed") with active, strong statements ("I am successful!"). Wishing opens the door to feeling bad about your current state, and that negative energy drags you down. Instead, stop wishing and live your vision now. Use strong, powerful statements and speak life into your purpose.

Shift #2: Let your actions speak louder than words. Our actions don't always reflect our goals. Think of a guy who says he wants to settle down and get married, but spends every night at bars flirting with different women. He sends himself and the world a mixed signal. Your thoughts absolutely must align with your actions.

Awareness is key. Identify the mixed signals you're sending, either in thought or speech. Write them down, cross them out, and replace them with statements that are in the present tense and that align with your desires.

B.A.L.A.N.C.E Technique #8:
Appreciation

> *"Gratitude unlocks the fullness of life.*
> *It turns what we have into enough, and more.*
> *It turns denial into acceptance,*
> *chaos to order, confusion to clarity.*
> *It can turn a meal into a feast,*
> *a house into a home, a stranger into a friend.*
> *Gratitude makes sense of our past, brings peace for today,*
> *and creates a vision for tomorrow."*
> *~ Melody Beattie*

There are so many things to appreciate—who you are, friends and family, important objects, circumstances, and events. I even believe it's important to appreciate the curveballs in your life—things that are annoying, hurtful, inconvenient, or bad in any other way.

In a moment of stress, close your eyes and visualize what you appreciate about yourself, others, something in your life, or a circumstance. You may decide to dedicate a section in your B.A.L.A.N.C.E. Journal to appreciation, where you can start listing the life aspects that you appreciate.

When one of my clients did this, she began with the obvious: her family, her friends, and her job. But then she went deeper and added things like: the smell of fresh laundry, the curl in my hair that I tried for years to get rid of, and the way my husband always makes sure the car has gas in it so I am never surprised by an empty tank. Her appreciation list grew and grew, and soon had hundreds of entries. Now, in her moments of frazzle, she looks at the list, focuses on what she has written, and sometimes even adds to it! Her stress levels have plunged, and her joyful feelings have mushroomed.

In my own life, too, the power of appreciation and gratitude is priceless. I am feeling kind of overwhelmed with gratitude at the moment, especially taking this moment to stop and think about the past year— just to name a few:

- My children have grown in leaps and bounds. Lulu is an artist.

She creates amazing jewelry, phone cases, artwork. She loves to craft and learn, and is already talking about applying for an arts high school. She uses her gifts in so many ways, and even has created art for charities. She marches to her own beat, loves her friends and family fiercely, and amazes us daily. And the Little Man creates comic book characters with detailed story lines, and has a whole plan to create a Netflix series, movies, and product lines out of them! He has an entrepreneurial spirit and dreams about directing movies and making video games. His characters are unique and so awesome!! He creates characters that he calls "unlikely heroes" that go against stereotypes. I love seeing what he comes up with every day!! He also is very smart, extremely kind, and looks up to his sister. I'm grateful for the way they do many things together. Yes, there is fighting, but there's also giggling, talking, teaching, and those moments make up tenfold for the wrestling on the floor.

• My husband is working so hard to provide for us, not just monetarily, but in so many ways, from helping with all the household stuff to surprising me with an iced coffee on a long day to being a kid at heart as he jumps and runs in the leaves with Lu and the Man. We may sometimes still be on Mars and Venus, but we always kiss each other goodnight.

• My parents are so amazing. They would do anything for anyone, and they are always willing to lend a hand or an ear, give encouragement, and believe in us. Their unwavering faith is such a blessing, and I am so grateful. From driving down at

A moment's notice when something comes up to surprising me with a beautiful card, everything they do is from the heart. And even though my parents worry about me still (they are the first ones I have to call whenever I land in a plane), I've learned to appreciate their concern.

• My mother-in-law is always thinking of us too. She does so many little things, and we are lucky to have her kind, generous heart. She raised her kids on her own, worked very hard all her life, and instilled that in my husband. I know he is the man he is because of his mother, and I am so thankful.

Appreciating the Curveballs and Imperfections

Appreciating life's curveballs is harder than giving thanks for the blessings, but it's so worthwhile to appreciate the storm that destroyed your fence, the fact that you were laid off, or your neighbors who constantly get on your nerves.

You're probably thinking, Why in the world would I appreciate

Chapter Five - A is for Add In and Appreciate

the bad things that have happened in my life? In my view, everything happens for a reason—even the bad things. And very often, the bad ends up leading to good.

My grandmother passed away almost eight years ago. It feels like yesterday, yet it also feels like a lifetime ago. My lulu and little Man and Niecey weren't even with us yet, and my husband and I were just friends at that time. My grandmother was amazing. She was a ballroom dancer who danced as long as her lungs allowed her to.

No matter how old I got, when I was in my grandmother's kitchen, I always felt like a little girl playing dress up as I donned her 1920s frocks, put on her pink Mary Kay lipstick, sang songs, and danced with her on the white tile floor.

She was a vibrant, positive woman who loved dragonflies. When her much younger friends would come over and complain about the usual stuff, my grandmother would say, "c'mon, ladies!" And push a button on her plastic flower pot that would sing and dance. She was the original inspirista.

The day my grandmother moved into hospice, family and friends gathered around her. The doctor said she had a few weeks left. That night, my mother and I stayed by her side. While my grandmother slept, my mom and I took turns getting coffee and vending machine snacks, crying, laughing, and talking. Early that morning, my grandmother passed away while my mom and I held her hands.

The sadness paralyzed me. I felt my back stiffen, and for three days I could barely move. The next few days were a blur. At the time, I had several guy friends whom I casually dated, but the only one who showed up for me was Michael. He and I were just friends, but his support in being there for me during a messy, uncomfortable, real-life moment made me see him for his heart. He even delivered a platter of food to my parents. Shortly after that, we began dating.

Almost a year later, Michael and I were married. Then in April, our lulu (her full name is Millana in honor of my beautiful, strong, inspiring Grandma Millie) was born. Two years later, our little Man came into the world and was photographed by my dear friend Jessica. In my favorite photo, he is hugging my husband's arm at the tattoo of all our names wrapped around a dragonfly.

Millana is now eleven and a half. She is an old soul, and reminds me so much of my Grandma Millie. The Little Man is nine and a half, and he just loves life so very much. The two of them exemplify the beauty of my Grandma Millie. I know we will all be reunited one day, but I do miss her so.

Here are a few of the lyrics from the song "I Hope You Dance" by Le Ann Womack that we played at our wedding in her honor:

> *I hope you never lose your sense of wonder,*
> *You get your fill to eat but always keep that hunger,*
> *May you never take one single breath for granted,*
> *GOD forbid love ever leave you empty handed,*
> *I hope you still feel small when you stand beside the ocean,*
> *Whenever one door closes I hope one more opens,*
> *Promise me that you'll give faith a fighting chance,*
> *And when you get the choice to sit it out or dance.*
>
> *I hope you dance....I hope you dance.*

I feel blessed by the beautiful imperfections that have happened in my life. They gave me strength and taught me so much more than any book alone can teach.

Often there are reasons for circumstances that we simply do not understand. I love to go back and connect the dots, tracing the good things that came as a result of the bad. Just knowing that allows me to have a greater appreciation for the cruddy things while they are happening.

Appreciate the Beauty of Being Heard

I want to share a story with you about a beautiful gift I received last Christmas. But, first, I will tell you a little of the backstory :)

As I mentioned, my grandmother was the 'original Inspirista'. She always had a smile on her face, loved with her whole heart, and danced up until her lungs wouldn't allow her to anymore.

My Grandma Millie and I were very close - she had such a huge impact on my life. I wrote about her in my previously released balance book, where I first shared the 'dancing flowers' story. I miss her every day.

Chapter Five - A is for Add In and Appreciate

My grandmother loved Christmas, especially Christmas Eve. She would have us all over her house, and she would serve her famous lasagna and baked chicken, we'd open presents, and spend the night just having fun together as a family. My mother has carried on my Grandma Millie's tradition, and I have to admit, it's hard not to think about her on Christmas Eve.

For the adults, we do a grab bag, so each family member gets a gift, something to open. Last year, I opened a special card from my Uncle Paul - that would have been enough because the message was so touching. But, then, when I unwrapped the box, opened the top, and looked down, my eyes started to play tricks on me - dancing flowers - my grandmother's dancing flowers were in the box!!

I could hardly believe it when Uncle Paul told me they were hers - the ones I wrote about in my book, the flowers that I always think of and can literally hear singing in my head whenever I feel like complaining. My eyes immediately welled with tears.

You know, I thought about why the gift touched me so much. Having this very special piece of my memories of my grandmother now again with me in my home is incredible. And, what also hit me, was the simple beauty of my voice being heard.

I think we all have a voice (our voice is the way we express ourselves and our love), and the way we express our individual voices is unique. Some people create stuff - jewelry, artwork, homes, songs, pies, you get my drift - and that is how they use their voice. When we appreciate or recognize what someone has created, it's kind of like acknowledging their voice. Listening to and hearing someone is an act of love.

Where is your voice? How do you express it?

My voice is in written words. When I was younger I wrote poetry, but now I write on my blog, or in my journal, or in this case, in a book. My Uncle taking the time to read my words and remember the stories made me feel heard and loved.

So, my challenge for myself and for you today is to 'hear' the people around us. What are they saying?

Acknowledge their voices. Listen with your heart and connect with theirs.

That really is the most beautiful gift we can give each other - after all, isn't this what life is all about?

Take Action
Appreciate the Moments, Big and Small, Good and Bad

Use a section of your B.A.L.A.N.C.E Journal just to keep an ongoing list of the things you appreciate about your life. Be specific, and know that it can be absolutely anything. You can write things like, "My socks feel so soft and warm fresh out of the dryer. My daughter kissed me on the nose. My dishes smelled so clean when I opened the dish washer." You get my drift. You can also begin to reflect on some of the messes and see what beauty came from them. It doesn't diminish the mess, it just brings some peace and gratitude for all life brings to us.

Chapter Five - A is for Add In and Appreciate

Summing Up

In this chapter, we talked about adding in to fill the space that's created by all the letting go you did in the previous chapter. Some of the things you'll add in to your life include:

Making choices every day that honor your core values

- Educating yourself about your body, your heart, and your mind
- Healthful, nurturing foods that energize and nourish you
- Passion for life and the beauty of miracles
- Time for you to nurture yourself
- A support team that can encourage you and help hold you accountable in ways that feel right for you
- Thinking about the importance of appreciation in a balanced life and brainstorming ways to pay attention to what really deserves your appreciation

In chapter 6 we'll discuss some fantastic navigation tools and strategies that will help you stay the course as you follow a journey toward a balanced, happy life.

Chapter Six
N is for
Navigate and Notice Nature

Instead of that anxiety about chasing a passion that you're not even feeling, do something a lot simpler. Just follow your curiosity. - Elizabeth Gilbert

When I was a little girl, my parents bought their first house. The inside of the house was an absolute disaster, but the minute my mother saw the backyard and the playhouse, she envisioned a beautiful home where my brother and I could run and play. The vision was so clear in her mind that she convinced my dad to buy the house, even though they had never renovated anything before.

When they moved in, my mother used her vision of the house as a guide every day, and with a very small budget, she and my father created the home of their dreams. They hit roadblocks along the way, of course—they even stripped fifteen different covers off of the countertop only to realize the counters were in horrible condition and needed to be completely replaced anyway. But they navigated their way through the challenges and built a beautiful home where we lived for most of my childhood.

If my mother had let fear cloud out her vision, she and my dad would not have purchased the home that brought us so many amazing memories. And if they hadn't worked so hard, it would not have become the place she envisioned it could be.

Like my parents, we all face challenges as we navigate our

Chapter Six - N is for Navigate and Notice Nature

way through life. When we have a vision for our life, we sometimes push it aside because we don't know how to make it happen. We may get frustrated with trying and choose to simply give up. Or we work too hard, we don't appreciate what's in front of us at the moment. We struggle and stress to make it happen quicker, because we think where we are is just not enough.

Now, there was a time in my life not too long ago that I believed we HAD to MAKE it happen. Whatever we wanted was the "it". And well, let's just say that life experience has taught me so much more than any textbook could. I do believe that with God, all things are possible. And I do believe that holding a vision of purpose for our lives and visualizing is extremely powerful. But, ultimately God really is in control. As I mentioned earlier in the book about 'appointments', sometimes God places us where we are for a divine purpose, even if it's not where we think we want to be.

That's not to say complacency is the answer. Complacency is the thief of potential. I believe God blesses the work we do to move forward despite challenging situations, even if His blessing isn't what we are (on the surface) hoping for. Deep beneath, the blessing is far greater. He blesses us for our faith, even if it's with just daily bread. And He blesses our patience. The thing is, He can move at lightning speed when necessary. Or we can be planted where we are for a season, or two, or several. Whereas navigating used to have a different meaning for me, now I see navigating as a way to rely on our anchor as a compass, and sometimes we are told to put the anchor down and rest. Sometimes, we have a vision of where we want to go, and the winds change so drastically, we are being re-routed. Sometimes we have to lose ourselves to find ourselves.

I've seen this time and time again, and I've experienced it myself. In this chapter, we'll look at the next of the B.A.L.A.N.C.E Techniques: navigating. During this chapter, I'll show you how to use your vision of purpose to release fear, to move forward with trust even when you don't know exactly where you're going, to commit to your core values by taking action, to learn when to rest, to know when to hand God the wheel, and to navigate detours along the way.

I'll also share some very effective navigational tools. First we'll talk about mini-goal setting and several fantastic ways to set the small, specific, everyday mini-goals that move us forward and open our hearts. I'll also tell you the importance of defining your success in ways that are purposeful and inspiring. Finally, I'll share some thoughts and tips about the wonderful value of noticing nature as you navigate through life. It's another B.A.L.A.N.C.E. Technique that is sure to bring you back to center during stressful moments.

Before we begin, I want to tell you a few things about navigating. I can absolutely help you figure out good ways for you to take inspired action in order to set and reach your goals. But I can't give you an absolute do-this, do-that blueprint.

When someone or something outside of you tries to navigate your life, failure is almost guaranteed. Only you can look within to find the steps that will allow you to successfully navigate this journey called life. And if you're setting goals, only you know yourself well enough to make a plan so customized that it will fit every part of your personality, schedule, core values, and lifestyle. But that doesn't mean you're on your own—absolutely not! Your wisdom comes from God, and He's the greatest teacher in town!

Sometimes women feel a little lost at this point. They want to be told exactly what to do. They want a blueprint. But let me tell you, I know from my own experience and the success of the women I've worked with that the only way to tap into your awesomeness, the only way to live a life in balance, is to look within yourself. So, in other words, you got this!

Once you accept that, navigating can actually be fun! Instead of being boxed in by a bunch of someone else's rules, you have the freedom to choose your own. You accept when you are being anchored instead of being anxious and impatient. You can hear God's redirection, and you move forward in a different direction with faith, even if you are fearful. Navigating and goal setting seems less like a race to be won and more like a journey to be enjoyed - more scenic, more serene for the most part, and yes, of course, at times, a bit crazy, too!

Although we put our trust in God, we still have to do the work, or at least accept His help in the form of earth angels. Did you ever hear the joke about the man who was on the Titanic? As the ship was going down, God sent several messengers to come help - one with a boat, one with a raft, and one with a helicopter. The man, as he was drowning, denied the offerings, saying, "I know my God will save me." When he finally drowns, the man meets God in Heaven. He asks God. "Why did you leave me? Why did you forsake me? Why didn't you come to save me?" To which God

Chapter Six - N is for Navigate and Notice Nature

replies, "What do you think the raft, the boat, and the helicopter were?" God doesn't want us to proverbially drown by just waiting. We have to act.

You can navigate your journey by taking small inspired steps and setting mini-goals. Planning ahead of time and holding yourself accountable will help you to gain a sense of accomplishment when you put your navigation plan in motion. And if, by tapping in to your innate wisdom, you discover you really like blueprints, you will be able to create your own. Just remember one very important thing: your core values (aka your "anchors") can be your compass. Allow your values to guide you, and always check your goals against your values to make sure they are in alignment.

Faith and Focus

I love watching tightrope walkers at the circus—their elegance, grace, and focus inspire such awe in me. (As an aside, I always think it's odd that we use the term three-ring circus to describe chaos. In reality, everything done in a circus is done with precision and laser focus—it has to be, or the performers would get hurt.)

We can learn a lot about life by observing circus performers, especially the tightrope walkers. They don't focus on the fact that they are a hundred feet in the air. They don't look at all the faces staring up at them and all the circus acts going on below them, and then freeze in fear of falling. Of course not. They take just one step at a time but keep moving forward to get to the other side.

They focus on the moment.

When we're doing multiple activities at once, we can't focus solely on the fact that we are doing so many things at once. This is overwhelming, and can lead to negative thoughts such as, I am stressed— I have too much to do. Or, I will never get anything done. Or, This is impossible!

Negativity gets you nowhere except stuck in a rut. If you have a laundry list of goals to navigate and tasks to get done and you are thinking about all of them, you can't focus on the task at hand. If you are at work and you're worrying about what to make for dinner, you'll spend more time on Google searching for twenty-minute chicken recipes than you will finishing the research you need for your presentation tomorrow. Then tomorrow morning, you'll stress about the un- finished presentation and focus more on the stress than on the task, which will lead to sloppy results.

The same is true when we are faced with a fear. I always feel far more in balance when I focus on faith instead of fear. Remember, having a positive attitude isn't just about what we say or how we present ourselves. For a positive attitude to be more than words, it must also be exemplified in our thoughts, our actions, and how we handle the situations we are presented with. It is a state of being. An attitude of faith permeates all areas of our life.

With an attitude of faith, you can have a laser focus on what you are aiming for, and then just move gracefully step by step, one foot in front of the other. When you focus on the task at hand and know that something else will follow soon, you're better able to keep moving forward.

This is true for anything you want to pursue in life, even the smallest of things, like driving someplace new. If you have a map with a final destination, you take the turns one at a time. If you jump ahead to the seventh turn before you've taken the first one, you're very likely to get lost. And if we miss a turn, or there's a detour, that's ok, too. With faith and patience, we ultimately will be shown the way.

Try to have the same laser focus as the tightrope walker. Walk through life with grace, elegance, and faith, even when you're facing fear, chaos, or even just a long to-do list.

Technique #9
Navigate: To Experience JOY in Your JOurneY

A few years back I met a man who had just opened his dream office. He said he had a big vision, and he knew exactly the furniture and light fixtures he wanted to have for the office; he knew the suit he would wear on opening day. He was focused and clear and worked 60-70+ hours a week, just to get to that next level, and earn the money he needed to buy the loft he envisioned and renovate it with all of the designer details. He talked nonstop to anyone who would listen about this office. He exhausted himself, and the 70+ hour work weeks soon turned to 80, When he was home with his family, his mind would still be working. His phone was close to his hand. He couldn't stop obsessing about opening this space and hiring a team of people.

Well, a few years after the vision began, he opened that office. He

Chapter Six - N is for Navigate and Notice Nature

did it!! He reached the goal!! He created the vision!! But...

He. Was. Miserable.

The day of the grand opening, he looked at the fancy light fixture, and he realized he lost two years of his life. Two years with his children making memories. Two years of dates with his wife. He didn't even know what was driving him. He said it began as a fun thought, but he got so caught up in making it perfect, that he missed the entire process. He melted down when everyone left the party. He felt awful, and like a failure - the opposite of how he thought he'd feel that day.

You see, our hopes and dreams and visions and goals should not just factor in our core values, our values should be woven into them. If your goal is making you not present with your family, and your family is one of your core values, something is amiss. Or if your goal is making you agitated and on edge with your friends, and you value human connection, it may be time to reevaluate your goals.

The beautiful thing about life, though, is it is forgiving. My friend now views his grand opening meltdown as a breakthrough instead of a breakdown. He immediately knew the changes he needed to make, and decided to slow down a bit. He began practicing presence, even meditating. He fueled his mind and his heart with powerful sources that aligned with his true self. He took breaks, started dating his wife again, and began spending much more time with his kids. His perspective, his vision, and his life transformed into something more meaningful, creating a joyful journey, not a race to the finish line.

Setting Mini Goals

If you've been racking your brain thinking about how to do something you want to do or how to As you are moving forward in life, keep this in mind: navigating should be fun! Give yourself permission to think outside the box, to consider possibilities, to try new things—you can even throw the map away sometimes. You can chart your own course. Open your mind, dig deep into your soul, be guided by your goals and core values, and create a path that will can serve as a guide to take you where you want to go. And have fun along the way!

Don't be discouraged if your journey is slow. Creating change is like rolling a snowball. At first, the snow won't pack, and no matter how hard you try, all you have is a pile of snowflakes. But, if you stick with it, soon, wow, watch out world! You are rolling a snowball bigger than you ever imagined.

When you want to make a change, release the burden of it. And then, choose to just do one small thing that is in line with your vision of purpose, and do it regularly. For example, if you want to start a small business using your gift of sewing, but the thought of finding time to do so is overwhelming you, release it. Instead choose to do something small that is in alignment with your purpose for opening the business. Maybe just sew a few minutes a day. Or if you have enough inventory sewn already, maybe start an online shop on Etsy, and list one piece at a time. Or keep a notebook in your purse to dream and plan whenever inspiration hits. Time passes anyway, so if it takes longer, at least you are moving forward.

Sometimes the small thing you do will inspire you to do a little more, and a little more. Sometimes it's just about creating habits around your goals. Think about brushing your teeth: doing it once in a while doesn't work. You have to do it twice a day, every day, or else your teeth decay. Think about relationships: you can't go on one date a year and expect to have a meaningful relationship with someone. True love grows from a steady stream of communication and connection. Think about careers, parenting, hobbies: all are most successful when the tasks to perform each are done regularly, consistently, and with passion.

And then, there are other times that God is just ready for your purpose to reach the world, and with lightning speed, He opens up space and time, lines up all the pieces behind the scenes, and boom, you're placed somewhere totally unexpectedly in a miraculous way. No mini goal could have gotten you there. No blueprint or mapped out plan could have made it happen. And there's no real way to recreate it or explain it.

All of this to say that when you are navigating life, you need to be flexible, faithful, patient. and open hearted. You can, of course, still set goals, have a vision, work hard, but don't forget your purpose, your values. And when you navigate from a place of trust and openness, God will take care of the rest.

Take Action
Mini-Goals: Setting One Small Goal at a Time

Setting mini-goals is an incredibly powerful process. Even the tiniest step or action, even if it's imperfect, will move you forward in some way. When you choose daily and weekly goals, you create momentum which brings vibrancy and energy into your life.,

Choosing mini-goals is an individualized process that must be based on your own personality and lifestyle. Your mini-goals reflect who you are and are different for everyone. For example, some women like very structured goals; others prefer open-ended goals. Some women write their goals down; others keep them in their heads. However, I always say give your thoughts power by putting them in motion—either by writing them down, speaking them aloud, or (this one is a must) taking inspired action. None of these strategies is best for everyone—you have to figure out what works best for you.

You may be wondering at this point how you know what mini-goal to set and what the heck inspired action means. Many women are used to a book telling them the goals they should go for. But I believe you have the answers within you. I find it quite amazing to watch women take the leap to trust themselves, be still and listen when they don't quite know the answers, and let their vision be their guide. Inspired action comes from listening. Spending quiet time to visualize and hear your inner guide helps navigation run smoothly.

Inspired action doesn't feel forced. It might not be simple and you may have to push yourself to do it, but it's coming from a deeper place within you. And even when something throws you off, you still choose to take the action.

Ask these questions to begin your navigation:

- What is my intention for today? For this week?

- How can I nurture my body, soul, and spirit?

- What step will I take today to move myself forward?

- Will I walk around my block one time?

- Will I write a letter to an old friend I have been thinking about?

- Will I read that book that's collecting dust on the shelf?
- Will I write a grocery shopping list and stock up on energizing foods?
- Will I eat more fresh vegetables, enlist a support team, or begin strength training?

Just do one thing and get that snowball rolling. You'll soon see how exciting it is to create change just by taking a single step!

By the Numbers

Some people write the date in numbers: 8/20/10. I like to spell it out: August 20, 2010. I don't know why, but there's something about numbers that drives me a little bonkers. Of course, they are a way of quantifying things, and they are probably more tangible for some people than words are. For example, many people define success by numbers: what a job pays, what's in their bank account, what the scale says, how many bedrooms are in their home, how many hours they worked in a day. I just don't define success that way.

Success to me is living with passion, energy, and purpose. Success to me is making sure I've kissed my husband goodnight every night, even on those nights when we're affected by the Mars-Venus thing. Success to me is having lunch with my daughter, reading her writings, or giggling with my son by dancing around the room with him. Success is being able to do a job I love and still have peace of mind to pay my bills and have some fun. And if money's a little tight, success is figuring out how to budget better, knowing what's important, and booking different types of work so it will be easier. Heck, some days, success is even just getting a shower, lip gloss, and matching socks on before leaving the house!

I understand that quantifying success makes it simpler for some people to measure themselves, but I think it makes it harder to figure out how to get where you want to be. I mean, sure, we can say, "I resolve to lose ten pounds," or "I want to make a six-figure salary," or "I want to be married only once." Hmmm . . . All good numbers. And, I understand, I used to also look at the end result—what I wanted in a numbers way. But, not being a numbers person, I always struggled with that perspective and was frustrated by how to get to those numbers.

Instead, I choose to use words to define what I really want for my life. Honestly, I don't care what the scale says, but I want to have tons of energy, feel great, and keep my body strong. Living well is a tool that helps me to do that. If the computer screen tells me I have X number of dollars in the bank, it doesn't really mean anything to me. But I'd like to take my kids on day trips, go on dates with my husband, save a little for the future, and give back to the world by helping others. If I have enough money—whatever the number—for that, I'm thrilled.

But, this is just me. Every one of us has our own way of viewing life, goals, success. I want you to tap into your personal definition in a way that feels weightless, without frustration, and honors your core values. Again, navigating is most natural when we are not getting caught up in it like a task to be conquered and done perfectly, but rather an exciting adventure, a joyful journey!

Take Action
Quiz Yourself: Which Goal System Works Best For You?

You may have no problem setting mini-goals for yourself, breaking it down into little daily actions, and holding yourself accountable. But for many women, it is more natural to navigate their kids' schedules or a work project than it is to navigate the vision of purpose they have for their life. Personal goals can sometimes feel frivolous or a big stretch to fit into a jam packed day. I understand completely! So I recommend four different strategies for navigating. You may want to give them all a try so you can see what feels best to you. And to make it even simpler to pick one to begin with, I've designed this Navigation Quiz.

Take the Navigation Quiz to figure out which navigation system may work perfectly for your personality type. Then we'll explore each type of navigation system.

1. My favorite program on the computer is:
    A. Microsoft Word
    B. Microsoft Excel
    C. Paintshop Pro
    D. What's a computer?

2. My favorite television show features:
    A. Stories about real people

B. How things are made
   C. People creating something from scratch
   D. I don't watch TV

3. My favorite subject in school is/was:
   A. Literature
   B. Math and/or science
   C. Arts and crafts
   D. Philosophy

4. I send birthday greetings with a:
   A. Handwritten message inside a store-bought card via mail
   B. Computer message, usually an e-card or typed via email
   C. Homemade birthday card created from scratch
   D. Letter or phone call

5. When I am packing for vacation, I:
   A. Go from room to room, looking around and deciding which items from each room have to be packed
   B. Print out a master packing list that I keep on my computer
   C. Sit down beforehand and write a detailed list of all the items I have to bring
   D. Just start tossing things in my suitcase—I know intuitively what I have to pack without really thinking about it

6. When planning a vacation to Italy, I would:
   A. Read a travel guide and write down a long list of places I want to see and restaurants where I want to eat
   B. Read several travel guides, use a yellow highlighter to mark sites of interest, and create a detailed itinerary for each day of the trip
   C. Read travel guides, but wait until I'm in Italy to decide where I want to go
   D. Skip the travel guides and explore whatever moves me when I step out of my hotel each day

7. My holiday shopping strategy is:
   A. Start picking things up as I browse through stores a few weeks before the holiday
   B. Order everything online and have it wrapped a month in advance
   C. Forget shopping—I create homemade gifts for friends and family
   D. I do all my shopping in one whirlwind day

8. I have an important meeting tomorrow. My strategy for figuring out what I'm going to wear is:
   A. The night before, I picture myself in the meeting and think about what would suit me best.
   B. I have several meeting outfits that I keep pressed and ready in my closet, so I grab one in the morning and get dressed.
   C. I spend twenty minutes the night before the meeting, mixing and matching various blouses, skirts, scarves, and jewelry and create a look that will fit the occasion.
   D. I glance in my closet in the morning, spend ten seconds picking something out, and get dressed without a second thought.

9. The spice jars in my kitchen are:
   A. In a spice rack on the wall or counter
   B. In their own spice drawer, organized in alphabetical order
   C. Located throughout my kitchen, stored with the foods they go with—for example, the oregano is on the shelf with the pasta and canned tomatoes
   D. Jammed into the cabinet over my stove

10. I file my tax returns:
    A. A few weeks before April 15
    B. In January, right after I receive my tax forms
    C. Whenever my accountant gets around to it
    D. Whenever I get around to it

If the majority of your answers are A, you are a words girl. You love to read and write. You love to hear people's stories and tell your own, so consider choosing story goals.

If the majority of your answers are B, you are a detail-oriented analytical thinker. You love checklists and calculators, and in school science probably made your soul stir. For a smart girl like you, consider choosing S.M.A.R.T. goals.

If the majority of your answers are C, you are a dreamer who sees potential in yourself and others. You are creative and visual, so consider choosing goals by visioneering.

If the majority of your answers are D, you are a deep thinker. You love studying philosophers and looking for the deeper meaning in things, so consider choosing intentions.

If your answers were all over the map, read through all the goal-setting strategies and choose what feels best to you. You'll probably end up mixing and matching a bit of each to create your own goal-setting strategy.

Story Goals: Navigate Your Way To Success By Telling A Story

Don't forget - no one else sees the world the way you do, so no one else can tell the stories you have to tell. - Charles de Lint

If you aren't quite sure what mini-goals will help you become the person you envision, you can create a story. To do this, set aside some quiet time, get comfortable, and open your journal. Let the blank page inspire you to see what your heart desires.

Write a story about yourself as you dream of being your most awesome self. Then begin to write about the steps you have to take to unleash that person. You can break it down a bit and write about what you'll have to do each week, and then each day, to fill the gap between where you are and where you'd like to be. Let the words pour out of you. Focus also on the benefits of your story goals. How will you feel when you awaken to your awesomeness? What changes might you see?

Give yourself time to think about story goals every couple of days. Each time you tell yourself your own success story, you'll envision more and you'll get more specific.
Here are some examples of story goals:

Today I am excited to walk five miles on the boardwalk. I can't wait to smell the fresh ocean air, feel the light morning breeze in my hair, and be warmed by the sun on my skin. Later, I will snuggle up on the couch and do some reading—this is a luxury I don't often give to myself!

I am in the mood to do a thorough cleaning of my office today, including the windows and desktops. My boss has been away, and I want it to look and smell nice when she returns next week. After work, I am going to the gym to do the elliptical trainer. I want to push myself, sweat, get my heart rate up, and feel my body working hard.

I know it's important to communicate better with my husband. I think today I will treat him the way I want to be treated instead of holding on to anger and resentment. Maybe I will surprise him by making him lunch and putting a note inside. He may think I've gone mad, but it's worth a shot at being romantic! I am going to spend time outside after everyone leaves—I think I will go for a long, brisk walk. Perhaps I'll even run a bit.

Be Smart with S.M.A.R.T. Goals

One way to keep momentum going is to constantly have greater goals. - Michael Korda

S.M.A.R.T. Goals are commonly used by authors, trainers, employers and coaches. S.M.A.R.T. Goal-setting is a proven, effective method for setting and accomplishing your goals. It is usually favored by people who like structure, although I've also seen some very freewheeling women warm up to S.M.A.R.T. Goals. To use this process, keep these S.M.A.R.T. Steps in mind as you create your mini-goals.

S is for Specific: Make your goals as specific as possible because specific goals are much more effective than general goals. They allow you to zero in on exactly what you want to achieve. For example, a general goal may be to exercise. A specific goal is detailed, targeted, and fully described: to walk for thirty minutes on the high school track five mornings a week at an intensity that elevates your heart rate to your target zone. Specific goals offer you a clear picture and an unambiguous story line that is easy to follow.

M is for Measurable: Be sure to establish concrete ways to track and measure your progress. For example, if your goal is to walk five days a week, use a calendar, chart, or spreadsheet to keep track of how frequently you walk, how long or far you go, and other details. This will give you a very clear sense of your progress and achievement, and you'll be able to easily track whether you've reached your targeted goals each day, week, month, quarter, and so on. When you meet your mini-goals, you'll see and feel your positive results in a way that inspires you to continue to work hard to live the healthy life you envision.

To make sure your goal is measurable, ask yourself questions such as: how long? How many? How much? How will I know when my goal is accomplished? Set realistic measurement periods—for example, keep a weekly walking log and evaluate
Your success every Sunday night. If you meet your goal,

congratulate yourself, spend a few minutes celebrating your dedication and enjoying how it feels to succeed, and then channel that positive energy into your next week's goal.

A is for Attainable: Set realistic, attainable goals that you can actually achieve. Unattainable goals are impossible to achieve and only cause frustration and negativity. For example, if you decide you'll walk one hundred miles in one weekend, and you haven't walked in years, not only could you fail to reach your goal, but you'll also feel bad for having failed. But if you set an attainable goal, you are in complete control. If you want to achieve it, you can. An example of an attainable goal is to start your weekend with a two mile walk and to eat at least five fruits and vegetables each day.

That's not to say you should set the bar so low you can't possibly fail. If you make goals too attainable, you won't feel excited and energized when you achieve them. Having lofty goals is a great idea—I firmly believe that just about anything is possible to a willing heart. But the best way to achieve a hard-to-reach goal is to break it up into smaller, attainable steps. If you've never run more than a mile and you decide you want to run a marathon, good for you! But don't expect to go from sedentary to athletic in one week. Instead, set a series of attainable mini-goals that will allow you to move at a steady pace toward achieving your larger goal.

If you commit to your vision, believe in yourself, and do the work, you can figure out the steps to make it happen. Think about the abilities, skills, resources, and attitude you need to create changes. You'll be amazed at yourself when a goal that once seemed out of reach has become your reality because you've stretched yourself.

R is for Relevant: Your goals have to be relevant and must mesh with your personality, your current state of mind, and the realities of your lifestyle. If you're a night owl, planning to get up at five a.m. every day to go to the gym is a goal that's destined to fail because it doesn't align with who you are. Set goals that take your life's realities into account.

T is for Tangible: a goal is tangible when you can see it, feel it, touch it, or count it. It is something real you can work toward, not simply an idea. There is less room for subjectivity when a goal is tangible. For example, setting a general goal to raise funds for an event is far different from setting a goal to enlist five people to each raise $200 in thirty days. They can accomplish their goal by selling twenty tickets each, less than one ticket per day.

S.M.A.R.T. Goals should answer the six W questions.

Who: Who is involved?

What: What do I want to create?

Why: Why is this important to me? What are the benefits?

When: Set your time frame. Hold yourself accountable.

Where: Establish a location.

Which: Identify your obstacles and strategize to overcome them.

I have worked with some women who create three S.M.A.R.T. Goals per week and others who create one or two daily. Choose what feels best for you. You may find that writing out your S.M.A.R.T.. Goals on Sunday sets you up nicely for the week ahead, or you may realize that writing your goal daily with your morning coffee revs you up for the day!

Create Your Vision by Visioneering

The key to realizing a dream is to focus not on success but significance—and then even the small steps and little victories along your path will take on greater meaning.
—Oprah Winfrey

We've already discussed the importance of having a vision that is connected to you in a profound, meaningful way. In chapter 2, you spent some time crafting a vision statement and a vision board. You may have even expanded upon your vision while reading the subsequent chapters. You can use your vision as a daily guide, looking to your vision for inspired action steps that will move you forward in creating it. I call this visioneering.

I love the visioneering method because it taps in to our innate power as human beings to literally create what we imagine.

Visioneering is deeper than just having the vision itself. More specifically, it is made up of four distinct components: vision, knowing, listening, and taking inspired action.

Go back to the vision of your life you created while brain dumping in chapter 2. Then try the following steps.

Schedule time to visualize. To some of us, visualization comes naturally. That's how it is with me. Visions appear when I wake up, in moments throughout the day, and before I go to bed at night. But that doesn't happen for everyone. When you're consumed by a packed schedule or repressed by the practical voice of a loved one, visualization can seem a little frivolous, almost like daydreaming. But trust me, it is far beyond daydreaming. A daydream is picturing yourself on a secluded island sipping a piña colada. Visualizing taps in to your core being, who you were born to be, and your best self.

Using your gifts and your talents, feeling awakened and alive right where you are on the grass that's beneath your feet in this moment. Waking yourself up to your vision gives you the permission to open your internal floodgates and let the vision out of hiding.

So if visualizing doesn't happen in a natural way for you, schedule the time to do it—when you wake up, at lunch, before you go to sleep. If you don't plan it, it may not happen. Start simply, with five minutes. After a while you'll start doing it naturally and automatically. Again, there really are no rules—you can close your eyes and think about your vision, write in your journal, or create a collage of pictures or a scrapbook. Pin pictures and notes to cork board in your bedroom or office; slip clippings and pictures into a photo box; or file goals, visions, and pictures neatly in an organizer. Do whatever makes your vision come alive for you.

Make it breathe with your knowing. A vision becomes more alive when you have a knowing around it. We not only hope and believe it will come to be, we know it will. It's in our hearts, it's in our being. When you fully commit and believe in yourself, you'll begin to know that you'll succeed. Remember, you are not trying to make your vision happen. You are simply being who you were born to be. Connect with your vision and commit to it.

Listen to your inner critic for a moment, and then tell her to take a hike. Notify your inner critic that she is no longer allowed to take up space in your brain. Don't repress her or sweep her under the rug. You are lovingly releasing her! When that inner critic voice takes you away from the state of knowing, it's like sticking a pin in a balloon. The vision loses its air, its power. Try to have a knowing with yourself the same way you would believe in your best friend. If your best friend was saying she was a failure, she was doubtful, she was unsure of her gifts in this world, you would probably go bananas telling her how crazy she sounded. Use your own internal knowing to do the same for yourself.

Listen to your heart. Listening is very powerful and often underestimated. I know sometimes we have a vision that we want so badly to make happen, that we go like gangbusters to succeed. But you can't bully a vision and ram it into action.

Vision flows gracefully, and the steps should be somewhat intuitive. How does a visioneer know what steps to take? Often just by listening. When you stop and listen—really listen—you open yourself to hearing something deeper that you may not have heard when you were running around like a maniac. Stillness is an action that gives voice to your inner wisdom.

I know you don't live in a bubble. And I completely understand that quieting your mind is much more easily said than done. But it gets easier with practice. Quiet your inner critic, breathe deeply, perhaps close your eyes and picture something serene, such as a white light, a blank canvas, or still water— and then just listen.

Take inspired action. You have created your vision, silenced your inner critic, and taken a moment to listen. You have a clear picture of the way you want to feel, look, communicate, breathe, be. Knowing all that, you can align your actions with your goals and take action inspired by your vision. By being what you see in your mind's eye, you fulfill your vision in a natural, organic way.

Throughout the day, stop and ask yourself if what you are about to do is in line with your vision of being balanced: Going for a walk? Yes, it is. Being stagnant all day? No, it isn't. Speaking kind words and being compassionate? Yes, it is. Yelling and getting frustrated at every turn? No, it isn't.

Visioneering is engineering your vision as you mindfully maneuver and navigate through life. Taking these four steps will help move the vision into your reality!

Change by Making an Intention

The secret of change is to focus all of your energy not on fighting the old, but on building the new. - Socrates

An intention is a powerful energy that we often don't realize we are using. Intention can direct your mind in an aware, conscious way. You put your decision in motion by putting it in words, followed by taking the inspired actions that support it.

Whenever I teach workshops, I ask the participants what their intention is with taking the class. Intention is more encompassing than the outcome, the goals, or even the objectives. Intentions are a way of being in the world. Using intention to navigate your journey is surprisingly powerful. You may begin to consciously state your intentions. And of course, they may at first seem more like goals or desires, but over time, your intentions will become clearer.

One woman on our last day of class ran in the door excited to speak to me before the others arrived. She exclaimed, "I get it! I know my intention. My intention is to be in balance!" She then explained that just by knowing her intention, she felt more in balance.

Intentions do not have to be overwhelming. As a matter of fact, a simple thought or statement can carry a lot of power, sometimes more than an entire paragraph can. Here are some examples:

- Today I will be kind and nurturing to myself and others.

- This week I will be plugged in to the world around me.

- I intend to live each day fully, to be powerful in body, mind, and spirit.

Another way to make intentions is to place an intention on something that will help keep you focused on your goals. One woman from the workshop did this when she was going to a wedding. She knew nobody on the guest list, and she worried that she would feel socially awkward and would soothe her anxiety by spending the evening eating. I suggested that when she entered the reception

Chapter Six - N is for Navigate and Notice Nature

room, she metaphorically place an intention on something in the room that reflected one of her core values and that she could relate to in a positive way. One of her core values is elegance, so she placed an intention on the gorgeous orchid centerpiece on her table. Throughout the evening, whenever she felt socially awkward, she looked at the orchid centerpiece and reminded herself that she could handle social situations with grace and elegance. The centerpiece was a talisman of sorts—something that could remind her of her intention whenever she needed a bit of support and encouragement. It worked like charm, so to speak—she got through the reception without feeling completely out of place.

Which navigation strategies should you use? Go with your gut. They should feel comfortable, and even if at first you have to work at navigating, once you begin, it should become a natural part of you.

Be Flexible When the Winds Change

When I was in high school, my family decided to take a road trip to South Carolina. My father is very reminiscent of Chevy Chase in the Vacation movies—he was super-excited, planned every detail, and had itineraries and road stops all mapped out ahead of time. What he didn't figure into his calculations was the fact that my mother, siblings, and I would all fall asleep during the ride, so he didn't have anyone to help navigate.

A couple of missed turns, and we were in the car for an extra couple hours. Now, I'm sure he wasn't the happiest when he was trying to figure out how to get us back on course, but we ended up near a unique place called South of the Border. In my father's original mapped-out plan, we would have missed it. As it turned out, our family had an absolute blast at the place that we may have never gone to if his plan had worked perfectly.

We are all a bit like Chevy Chase (and my father) as we plan our life journey. We pick a destination and head straight for it. But sometimes we get lost and the best, unexpected things happen. When we're blown off course, we learn lessons, we connect more with each other and with nature, and we often find happiness.

It's great to have a vision—knowing where we want to go and taking the steps to move towards it. But the next time your road map takes you on a detour, trust in the absolute power that life has a beautiful way of unfolding perfectly as it should.

B.A.L.A.N.C.E. Technique #10:
Noticing Nature

As you know, my B.A.L.A.N.C.E. Techniques are designed as a way to find balance during stressful moments. You've learned to stop to breathe, accept, laugh, and appreciate. Now it's time to notice nature. It's easy to get wrapped up in the hustle and bustle of life, but if you are in a bit of a funk or feeling stressed out to the max, take notice of the nature that surrounds you. You are bound to lower your blood pressure, calm your body, appreciate more, and even learn a lesson or two.

And what you notice in nature actually holds a mirror up to what is within you already. Twenty people may look at the same view and each see something completely different. You can discover much about yourself just by looking at the world around you. Not only is it soothing to watch a bird fly, to smell a flower, to stare at a starry sky, but it is also a way to learn a bit about ourselves.

Sitting on my front porch is one of the great joys of my life. Today I focused on all the beautiful foliage right across from our home. We don't live in a secluded area—in fact, the highway is just a few turns away. And yet, there is so much natural beauty right outside my door. As I enjoyed the leaves, this quote popped into my heart:

> *Adopt the pace of nature; her secret is patience.*
> *—Ralph Waldo Emerson*

I can't even imagine how old they are, how many stories they have to tell, the sage trees that surround our home. Nature is patient.

There are many things in my life that I want to unfold, and I'm sure the same is true for you. You may remember Veruca's famous line from Willy Wonka and the Chocolate Factory, "I want it now!" We may not stomp our feet, but I think we all feel like Veruca sometimes, especially when we have our minds made up about something. But patience is a virtue. We shouldn't wait in anticipation for life to happen. It happens naturally as it should, moment to moment. And, as Emerson points out, we must adopt

Chapter Six - N is for Navigate and Notice Nature

the pace of nature.

Today it dawned on me that the trees are all imperfectly gorgeous and unique. Nature is beautiful, but not perfect. The trees don't lineup standing the same height wearing the same shade of brown. They are scattered, their branches varying in size, shape, and color. They are chipped, worn, and spotted. Nature is flawed perfectly.

There are so many lessons right before our eyes if we just open them and take a look around. Today, think of something you've been wanting, anticipating, and let it go. Let go of the need for perfection. Trust everything will all work out in time, and enjoy each moment.

Obstacles and challenges are a natural part of life. No one is without them, and they can pop up anywhere, anytime, and often when we least expect it! Nothing goes perfectly as planned. But YOU can handle anything!! And remember, God's power is made perfect in our weakness...

Think about it, you may look at the Palm Tree and think it's kind of flimsy, right? But in its perceived weakness lies its strength - the Palm Tree is even stronger than the Oak Tree! Yes, the Oak has a sturdy appearance, but because of the Palm Tree's agility and flexibility, when storms and strong winds come, it can bend!

Like a butterfly, change is the essence of life. Be willing to surrender what you are for what you could become.

There are so so many lessons, too many to mention, and we each derive our own lesson based on our current state. Ten of us can see the same butterfly fluttering past us, and each takes away our own lesson from it.

One of us may see beauty in what's delicate. Another may see perseverance and strength. Another may notice the unique beauty butterflies bring, as no two are the same.

For me, when I see the butterfly in this moment, I think that cocooning is normal and necessary for growth and development. You will know when it's time to shed some layers, and emerge into the world weightless and ready to fly. Your spirit will awaken & you will be the magnificent person who you were born to be.

And in a few years, months, even weeks, days, or moments, I may learn a different lesson when I see a butterfly, as we are in a constant state of growth and change ourselves.

I'll never forget about eight years ago, while the Little Man and I were out food shopping, Michael and LuLu were on our front porch. A caterpillar was crawling at Lu's feet. According to Michael, she jumped about a mile high. She was scared, and didn't want it to crawl up her leg. Michael explained to her that the caterpillar is her friend, and just because she's small and furry, she needs to be loved, too.

Lu let Michael place the caterpillar in the palms of her hands. After she examined it, she noticed its beautiful and gentle nature. She talked to it for a few minutes, apologizing for her fears. She even gave her a name, "Rainbow Heart".

When the Man and I arrived home, Lu was still holding the caterpillar. In a soft, yet ecstatic voice, she said to us, "Mommy! Brother! Meet my new friend!!" Michael had just snapped a photo of her with Rainbow Heart:

We sat on the porch for a bit longer, then finally let Rainbow Heart go. We went inside to have some dinner. She went on and on about how she was scared, but realized there was nothing to be afraid of, and how she couldn't wait to meet more new friends.

About a half hour later, Michael went back on the porch. He called for me loudly, and as I looked up at the glass door, I was amazed. Rainbow Heart inched her way up the door, and was planted right in the center. Lu and Man danced in circles around the living room singing, "She's back! She's back!" We went on the porch to say hello again to her.

I started to think about caterpillars, and what they mean. Caterpillars are a symbol of the beginning stages of transformation. They symbolize preparation for growth.

Then, suddenly it dawned on Michael and I how magical it actually was for Lu and Rainbow Heart. You see, that following week, our little girl was going to school for the first time. She was changing, growing, blossoming right before our eyes. I had been fearful, nervous, even sad at times, while also proud and excited, of course. The mixed emotions of this change surely went away as I realized Rainbow Heart came to prepare our little LuLu for her next phase of life.

Chapter Six - N is for Navigate and Notice Nature

And don't you know, six years later, the week before Lu was going to Intermediate School, I thought my eyes were deceiving me; a caterpillar was planted right in the middle of our front door, almost the exact spot that Rainbow Heart inched up to. Michael and I recalled the incident from years before right away. The Little Man even slightly remembered. We were all in awe of nature's ability to calm us, remind us, and be there for us.

Connecting with Nature Daily

Our Little Man amazes us. Since he was able to run, he's always loved to run around our front yard. He sometimes has his ball with him as he bounces it around the sidewalk, but more often it's just him, his running shoes, and the ground beneath his feet. He runs up and down and all around, and his imagination is right there with him. Sometimes he's on a battleship protecting us from warriors in the sky. Sometimes he's in the desert trying to find water. Sometimes he's making a 40-yard dash to win the game.

He's had so many good falls in our front yard, scraped knees, bumps, even sometimes a bruise. But, it doesn't stop him from going back out there the next day and having his time to run and play in nature. I remember one day I was working on a project, and I knew I wasn't able to pay full attention, so I asked him if he could play inside instead of outside. He looked at me with those big eyes, and said, "Momma, I want to get my energy out."

And so I replied, "Can you get your energy out inside? I am in the middle of a project, and I can't go outside right now."

He said, "It's just not the same. I like to be in the air." And then it dawned on me, he gets his energy out, but also takes energy in from nature. While air *is* oxygen and of course air is inside too, the outdoors is "his oxygen" that he needs to connect with daily. And for some reason, it felt good in my heart, I totally understood, put the project down, and went outside with him.

I needed the nature break, too.

Take Action
Give Yourself a Nature Break

Take time each day to connect with nature. See what you notice around you. Look at everything, the blades of grass, the dirt, the trees, the birds, even the bugs, Whatever you see around you, take note of. What pops into your heart as you are noticing nature? You may jot it down in your B.A.L.A.N.C.E Journal if it's something you want to reflect on later, or just "be" with nature and connect with the air, the sky, the ground. And it doesn't have to be for hours, sometimes just a few moments give you a fresh perspective, a clear mind, or a lesson needed.

Something Fun
Run A Rainy Day Milk Bath

Lulu, Little Man, and I often go to our front porch when it rains. We love just watching the rain fall. The kids are calmer on the porch when it rains—it relaxes them. And it is such a wonder to witness the drops covering the blades of grass and flower petals in uniquely beautiful patterns; the sound is soothing to our ears.

I think rain gets a bad rap. Sure, it may cause delays when you're traveling or create frizz in a freshly blown-out head of hair, but I think it is nature's way of telling us to stop and breathe. It's fun to embrace the rain, and when it's a soft rain, I like to relax right along with it. Sometimes a rainstorm inspires me to take a milk bath using a simple homemade mix that has healing benefits to the body.

Makes 1 bath.

What You'll Need
2 cups whole milk 1 cup sea salt
1 cup baking soda

Let's Do This
In a large bowl, mix together the milk, sea salt, and baking soda. Run your bath to a warm temperature, and pour the mixture in. Set a serene mood by lighting candles and turning off the light switch. Leave the books on the bookshelf and turn your mind off.

Open your windows, let the breeze flow through, and just listen to the rain. Milk has natural softening and soothing properties. (Cleopatra knew this—she took frequent milk baths to keep her skin fresh and beautiful.) Milk contains lipids that deeply moisturize the skin. Sea salt helps improve circulation, assists in rejuvenating the cells, and completely relaxes the body. Baking soda is known as a detoxifier that helps you feel reenergized and has an alkalizing effect that counters the acidity typically caused by red meats,

Chapter Six - N is for Navigate and Notice Nature

cheese, sugar, and refined foods. All those benefits, plus soft skin and relaxation too!

Summing up

In this chapter, we talked about the following navigation strategies:

- How to use your vision to navigate your way through challenges and obstacles with joy
- The importance of setting mini-goals
- Four powerful goal-setting strategies that can guide you in customizing goals to your personality, schedule, and way of looking at life: story goals, S.M.A.R.T. Goals, visioneering, and intentions
- Ways to find motivators that energize rather than drain energy

In chapter 7, we'll determine what specific obstacles may get in the way of achieving your goals, identify surefire ways to confront them, and formulate a plan that you can use to set out clear, specific ways to hold yourself accountable to your goals and vision.

Chapter Seven
C is for
Confront and Connect

*Nothing ever goes away until it
has taught us what we need to know.* - Pema Chodron

When I was little, I loved bowling. My parents began taking me to the lanes as soon as I was old enough to stand, and they let me have a go at it. Back then there were no bumpers in the gutters, but it didn't matter. The fact that I got to roll the ball made me happy, and even if no pins fell, I would jump up and down and make a happy fuss.

As I moved from bowling for fun into a kids' league, I started to take it more seriously, and I only wanted to get strikes or spares. Of course, I would miss sometimes, and it would really make me mad. Instead of a happy fuss, I made a mad one.

I'll never forget my father's words after one of my meltdowns when I said I was giving up the sport. I was sick of not being able to break 100.

"Jennie, great bowlers become great bowlers because they love the game. They hone their skills, they get gutter balls, and they learn from their mistakes. They mess up, but they never give up."

That lesson has stuck with me in many ways throughout my life, and I think of it whenever something doesn't go as planned. Love the journey. Keep working, learning, experiencing, and most importantly, keep going.

Life is full of obstacles and challenges. You hit a traffic jam on the way home from work. You plan to make a salad for dinner and realize you're out of lettuce. As you run out the door to an art class

Chapter Seven - C is for Confront and Connect

you just signed up for, your daughter unexpectedly tells you there is something you have to go to at the school. Life throws plenty of big obstacles at you too—job layoffs, health problems, the end of a marriage, the loss of a loved one. And then there are the obstacles that come from deep inside you—fear, self-doubt, despair, resignation. All these obstacles can throw you off balance and distract you from fulfilling your goals and your life vision.

Obstacles are an inevitable, unavoidable part of life. But that doesn't mean you are powerless when they occur. In fact, if you put yourself in the right frame of mind, you actually have way more power than you realize to cope with all kinds of challenges. You truly do have power within you to confront life's obstacles and stay in balance—or if they knock you off your feet, you have the power to pick yourself up and begin again on your journey of living a happy, healthy life.

In this chapter, we'll talk about how to confront your challenges, harness your inner power, and prevent obstacles from throwing you off balance and that block you from your light.

First, we'll work on defining the obstacles that prevent you from meeting your goals. To do this, we'll use some terrific tools, including the energy sappers exercise, which will assist you in identifying what is depleting your energy—including life's incompletes and tolerations. Then, I'll give you tips on how to surmount your obstacles by confronting the source of your roadblocks head-on.

At the end of the chapter, I'll explain the value of connecting, another B.A.L.A.N.C.E. Technique that will help you find strength from others as you face all of life's obstacles.

B,A,L.A.N.C.E Technique #11
Confront: To Overcome Obstacles and Resolve Root Issues

One day while I was folding laundry I heard my Little Man in his room playing. He is very into Ninja Turtles at the moment, so it's common place to hear him talking like Michelangelo (or as he lovingly calls him, Mikey the Jokester), and jumping around doing karate kicks. He has an orange bandanna mask that he sometimes wears when he's really in the mood to "play the part". When I opened his door, I literally laughed out loud. I guess he couldn't see his bandana which was on top of his dresser, so instead he was wearing orange gym shorts on his head.

I love the creativity and inventiveness (is that a word?) of children. They have a vision (in this case, being Michelangelo), they have an obstacle or challenge creating it (unable to find the real bandana), they keep going (and use shorts instead).
Simple wisdom.

As I mentioned earlier, obstacles are a natural part of life. No one is without them, and they can pop up anywhere, anytime, and often when we least expect it! Think about it, you're driving to work right on schedule, and BAM, a detour pops up in the middle of the road. You are looking forward to a romantic night out with your sweetie, when he/she storms in the door after a horrible day at work.

Yes, don't I know it, obstacles and challenges occur ~ nothing goes perfectly as planned. The thing is, since all life is a lesson, we can learn a lot about ourselves by examining the obstacles we've already faced. You might want to write down an example of when you overcame an obstacle. Here are a couple of questions to consider: How did you handle the challenge? How did you go over, break through it, or work around it? What inspired you to continue moving and/or confront the roadblock?

Awareness is always a key tool in discovery. Just acknowledging and recognizing your obstacles (if they are holding you back), can be very insightful. Using the "Over, Through, or Around" technique, gives us a simple framework for moving forward. I usually question myself with the challenges I am facing that weigh me down - do I want to work over, through, or around this obstacle?

Sometimes we don't really have a choice - if we want to move forward, we have to work over it, or work around it, or work through it. Sometimes trying to work around it really {if your honest with yourself} isn't in fact working, in which case we have to work through it. Sometimes, there is no working through it, we need to re-route if we want to move forward, take a detour and work around it, like my son putting the shorts on his head. You get my drift.

These are all very personal choices, and the thing is {NEWSFLASH}, we're not perfect, we all make mistakes, especially when we are being challenged, and that's ok. We can learn from them, grow from them, and often, we discover a deeper meaning from them in this beautiful gift of life. But the point is, we don't

Chapter Seven - C is for Confront and Connect

give up and stop moving.

We can pause, of course, take a beat to listen to our heart - sometimes I think maybe the setback is intentional, God wants to move me somewhere else, I just need to get out of my own head and listen to the direction. I can't help but think of the story of Jonah in the belly of that big fish during the crazy storm...he was probably terrified flailing around inside a whale?? But, as the lesson goes, the whale actually saved his life.

Take Action
Identify the Best Method for Facing an Obstacle

Inventorying past successes helps us discover a lot about ourselves. Grab your B.A.L.A.N.C.E Journal, and think about obstacles you have faced over your lifetime:
- Write down an example of when you overcame an obstacle.
- How did you handle the challenge?
- How did you go over, break through it, or work around it?
- What inspired you to continue moving and confront the roadblock?
- Repeat this exercise for as many obstacles as you can recall.

Inventorying your current obstacles is helpful. List out some common obstacles that occur in your life or current obstacles or challenges you are facing now.

Acknowledging them may begin the process of resolving them naturally. Always do this in a way that feels comfortable to you, and enlist support of a professional if necessary. In your B.A.L.A.N.C.E Journal, create a page that just says "Currently, these are the obstacles I am facing:" and list them out.

You can't confront your obstacles if you don't know what they are. So take some time to identify what's getting in your way on your journey toward balance. Spend a few minutes at the end of each day looking at the goals you set for the day and tracking whether you achieved them. Then ask yourself about the goals you didn't meet. What got in the way? Were your goals realistic? Did you schedule enough time to do the tasks on your list? What (or who) interfered with your ability to do what you planned to do?

Confronting is not about creating conflict, but rather about creating peace by identifying, facing, and resolving obstacles and root issues that have been weighing heavy on us, hence throwing us off balance.

Write your daily barriers and obstacles in your B.A.L.A.N.C.E. Journal for a week or two. Then go back and look for trends. Does one particular obstacle keep popping up? Does the same problem get in your way day after day? Analyze why these things keep happening. Are you saying yes when you should be saying no? Are you being unrealistic about your schedule, about how much time you have, and about how much time tasks take? Are you keeping your schedule in your head instead of writing it down in a reliable planner?

Working Over an Obstacle Sometimes we want to just get rid of an obstacle, but we realize it just 'is what it is', it's going to be there, but we have to keep working 'over' it. What is an obstacle that is beyond your control that you have worked over, that you are working over currently, or that you need to work over?

Working Through an Obstacle Sometimes we want to hide an obstacle, but we realize it just keeps popping up like a whack a mole. We try to stuff it down, but it's not going away. We have to confront this obstacle head on, and work through it to alleviate it. What is an obstacle that needed to be worked through (and YOU DID!) or that are working through currently, or that you need and want to begin working through?

NOTE: Working Through Obstacles is difficult, and may require enlisting proper support through the process. There are many resources available, so always remember to reach out for help when necessary. We are not meant to walk this journey alone!

Working Around an Obstacle There are obstacles that we can avoid, simply because we've learned from past experiences. At one point, you either worked through the obstacle or worked over the obstacle, so now you have the knowledge and first-hand experience to work around it! What are some obstacles that simply did not affect you in any way because you had a Plan B or a work-around already in place? What are some obstacles you've learned from that you would like to note now so you are prepared for the future in case something similar pops up again?

Chapter Seven - C is for Confront and Connect

Confronting Serious Problems

If you are struggling with deep-seated emotional issues such as uncontrolled eating disorders, major relationship conflicts, trauma, abuse, unresolved grief, clinical depression, or other mental health problems, you probably need more help than a book can give you. If so, please seek help from a psychologist, therapist, grief counselor, or other mental health care provider. These trained professionals can help you confront painful issues in a safe, constructive way.

Some Common Obstacles

Of course, there are so many types of obstacles we face on a daily basis. Women are so resourceful, we often don't even need to journal them, because we work through them in the moment! I find that there are some common obstacle themes which I narrowed down to four categories - all of these four present themselves in dozens of ways. But overall, these tend to be the biggest roadblocks for most women:

1. Overscheduling and overcommitting to activities

2. Lack of communication at home and in the workplace

3. Becoming so preoccupied with the little things in life that you don't have time or energy to think about the bigger picture.

4. Under-prioritizing yourself and the gift of life

Once you identify your obstacles, you can figure out what to do about them. Do you need a new scheduling system? Do you need to find a method of communication that works better for you? As you analyze your everyday obstacles and brainstorm solutions, start making changes in your daily goals. Continue to keep track of what you achieve and what you don't, and make specific plans for what to do when certain obstacles arise. Soon you'll start to have much more control over your everyday obstacles.

A great way to turn everyday obstacles into opportunities for change is to create your ideal schedule. This is a fun activity, and very helpful! On a blank calendar, fill in your ideal schedule. Create it without limitations or obstacles. (But be realistic—you can't just go to the spa all day.) Remember to factor in your life vision, your day design, and your core values. Think about the gift of each day and how you would like to spend it.

If you have children, remember time is a gift to them too. If they are scheduled to the hilt with activities, they aren't able to appreciate sitting around the table having a family dinner, lying in the grass, or playing old-fashioned games like Monopoly or Bingo.

Designing your ideal schedule will allow you to include activities you want to do but think you don't have time for, and it may very well lead to transforming what feels like a daydream into a reality.

Sometimes just the awareness around what you want, sets the intention in motion.

This happened with Sandy, who said she wanted to do more volunteer work. She loved volunteering, but months and sometimes years would go by without her doing any volunteer work. She was so busy with her kids and work and everything in between that she couldn't find time. She also thought it would be good to get her kids involved in some volunteer activities.

In Sandy's ideal schedule, her kids' after-school and evening activities were limited to Mondays and Wednesdays. That would leave Tuesday and Thursday evenings open, giving Sandy and her children time to volunteer at the senior center or the children's hospital. Her ideal schedule also made room for her and her family to prepare a home-cooked meal at least one night a week. And it included time for her to go to the gym and to relax with her friends. Sandy's ideal schedule was much different from her real life, but by simply going through the exercise of imagining an ideal schedule, Sandy became excited about taking better control of her life.

Over the next few months, Sandy consciously thought of her ideal schedule and how she could change her family's current schedule accordingly. She spoke with her husband about her desire to hit the gym early in the morning, and he was all for it! He knew she felt better when she exercised. As it came time to enroll/re-enroll her kids in activities, Sandy helped her children decide which were most important and which could be dropped. With fewer activities, Sandy found time at least twice a month to volunteer, either by herself or with her kids or husband.

Another way to confront your everyday obstacles is to change the

Chapter Seven - C is for Confront and Connect

way you communicate about your time. If you need to change the way you value and use time, be sure to share this information with the people in your life so they can understand and honor your needs.

The way you value your time often reflects the way you value your-self. And the way you value yourself often is reflected back in the way others value you. This often isn't conscious, and many people don't even realize they are doing it—it just happens organically among us.

When we share and communicate openly, we change the energy of our relationships, and we change the energy we carry within ourselves, which in turn creates a more confident self.

In order to reflect a different message about yourself and your time, you must be clear about what you want. Before opening up discussion with others, write about it in your B.A.L.A.N.C.E. Journal.

Let's say you are working more than you want, and it's affecting your relationship with your family and yourself. You want to tell your coworkers that you need a break. Write out what you want from the situation:

I am exhausted. I work day and night, and it never feels good enough. I feel like a pancake spread too thin. I have no time for me, no time with my family, and you constantly e-mail or call even after I've left work. I just want some time to relax and be with my kids and my husband. Can you please give me some space? You are overbearing, and you expect way too much from me as an employee.

Read it back as if you were the recipient of the information, and hear it as though someone is telling it to you. Does it sound harsh? Are you immediately on the defensive? If so, reframe it in a positive, productive way. There's probably some great information in there that may be clouded by insults or venting.

Remember, the goal of communicating effectively is not to belittle or to blow up. The goal is to change the way the recipient views and values your time. If an overbearing boss doesn't let you sleep at night because your blackberry is ding-ding-dinging, remember you taught him that it was okay to do that by answering the call, even if you only answered once. Be honest, acknowledge the positive, acknowledge your part in the miscommunication, and then state what you are choosing. According to licensed psychotherapist and relationship expert Tom Kersting, the way in which a message is delivered to the recipient (in this case, your boss) is perhaps more important than the message itself. Tom told me, "The majority of folks, including bosses, are defensive by nature, so the delivery of your message must strike a positive chord with your recipient so that the walls of defensiveness do not emerge." He even shared a script with a better way to communicate your message:

I have been thinking about my wonderful life over the past few weeks, and although I appreciate all that I've been blessed with, I am exhausted. I feel like a pancake spread too thin. I love my job so much that I find myself continuing to work from home in the evenings when I should be unwinding, reading to the kids, and spending quality time with my spouse.

I know that I'm always quick to respond to my blackberry, and that is my fault. My engrossment in work has taken its toll on my family, and on me, so I've decided that I need to dedicate my time after work exclusively to my family. Doing so is not only right, it gives me fulfillment, and the more fulfilled I am, the more productive I can be at work. From now on, I am going to turn my blackberry off after work, my kids are going to turn off the television, my husband is going to turn off the computer, and we are going to spend time together the way a family should.

Your Circles of Life

We tend to compartmentalize our lives into separate areas. Family is in one bucket, career is in another, health is in another, and so on. But that's not how it is in real life. If you're worried about your career, it impacts your relationships. If you're constantly butting heads with your teenage son, it affects your ability to nurture your creative side. When any one of these life areas is out of balance, it can drain energy from all the others. It's not easy to put your finger on the root issues you are facing. They often have nothing to do with what it seems on the surface at all. That's why it's important to build a strong core values system - the stronger you are in the center, the less likely little things will throw you off balance as a whole, and the bigger things are a bit less challenging when you have strong anchors. It's important to look at your whole life as you set out to identify the obstacles that trip you up. Referring back

Chapter Seven - C is for Confront and Connect

to the Balanced Inspirista graphic in Chapter 2 can help.

We can learn so much about ourselves just by looking at the different areas of our lives, including our surroundings. I remember moving into my first apartment like it was yesterday. I walked in, laid down on the floor, and decided to paint the room orange. I was feeling happy and independent, and orange felt like a good fit.

After about six months of living on my own and going through some tricky times with relationships—listening to too much Tori Amos and developing a taste for Modigliani's artwork—I painted my orange walls deep plum. When my mother saw the room, she seemed quite concerned. "is everything okay?" She asked.

I guess I was in a funk and didn't really see it until my mother asked me about my decor. The funk had a deeper effect on me than just the color of the walls, though. I realized that even though the scale was down, I suddenly wasn't nurturing myself. I again wasn't feeling good enough, I ate very little in fear of gaining weight, I stopped enjoying food that I loved so much, and I focused so much on food that it became my adversary. Even though years before I had learned that self-love was the key to being healthy, I suddenly wasn't being kind to myself or my body anymore. My surroundings reflected this.

Often the choices we make about our living environment, clothes, and hair reflect what we're thinking. But having deep-plum walls and mopey artwork magnified my sadness, and I lived up to my own expectation of being a woman scorned. I ate less, feared weight gain tremendously, and began avoiding full-length mirrors again. I was clearly not in balance or appreciating my body, my gifts, or my life. Even though I was in the beginning stages of helping women become healthier, I realized by my deep-plum walls that I was once again struggling to find balance and completely forgot my own awesomeness.

The community of women I surrounded myself with came to my rescue. While I was trying to find my balanced self, many of my friends and clients lifted me up. My business was decorated in a very inspirational way—phrases on the walls and encouraging words everywhere. Frenchie, a dear friend and client, noticed I wasn't myself. One day, she asked what was going on, and I released a little on her, just dumped out the dating disasters I was having. She smiled at me, a deep, loving smile, and simply pointed to the words I picked out myself that were in frames and on the walls that were chosen to inspire others. She knew I could use the encouragement and inspiration that day. Frenchie's simple concern was just what I needed.

I know that being surrounded by positive energy in the form of people, words, music, memories that make me smile, and images of dreams for my future have made all the difference in how I nurture and care for my body, how I have overcome obstacles and challenges in my life, and how I have been able to help others do the same.

You may not have changed your wall color or taken any other drastic measures, at least not that you are aware of yet. But using my Balanced Inspirista graphic will help you define obstacles and barriers in every part of your life. Notice that surrounding the inspirista are the eight circles that make up most people's lives:

1. Relationships: The dynamics, effects, and growth of all personal and business relationships

2. Physical Environment: The space you're in at home, in your office, in your car, and elsewhere in your world

3. Personal Development: a clear path of development as it relates to your relationship with yourself and others

4. Fun and Play: activities that support self-expression

5. Finance: Your concerns about money

6. Career: The many aspects of your work life and career path

7. Wellness: The various aspects of your physical, mental, emotional, and spiritual health

8. Gifts and Creativity: That which makes your soul stir

Remember, that while the circles of life are "surrounding" the Inspirista, the circles of life still are interrelated. You are in the center. All the circles pass through you, and what happens in one circle goes through you and impacts the other circles. In my case, bad relationships impacted my physical environment, my physical environment then impacted my relationship with myself, and my relationship with myself became less than nurturing, impacting my wellness. The impact each circle has on the other varies from person to person, so you may want to create your own, noting your specific life circles and intertwining those that impact each other.

Also remember from Chapter 2, your overall balance is made up of not only your lifestyle factors but also your internal muscle, your body, and your caring balance—so the stronger you are in the center of your world, the less impact each out-of-balance area may have on other areas of your life.

Unidentified Hidden Obstacles (UHOs) can mess with your life balance UHOs are tricky to identify because they are the root (or source) of the challenge. The UHO is usually different from the symptom that is presenting itself to you. A symptom may be unhappy relationships, trouble with finances, or even lack of time. If you focus only on the symptoms, your obstacles will keep popping up like a Whac-A-Mole. But if you treat things at the root or source, you get to a deeper resolution with them. Boy, do I know this is hard, as there are many things in my own life I am still trying to understand the root cause for. I do believe though, we are blessed for bringing our cares to God and He helps us so greatly with His grace and mercy, even if we feel like a total mess.

Once you identify the UHO, you can essentially stop simply treating your symptoms. And what's more exciting is that in most UHOs, there are extremely valuable lessons to be learned about ourselves and our lives.

You may be getting tripped up by unidentified hidden obstacles if:

- You're not meeting the goals you set
- Your tools don't seem to work
- You have trouble moving forward and creating a vision
- You aren't living up to the vision you set for yourself
- You are getting frustrated or angry with yourself
- You have trouble meeting your mini-goals
- You feel stressed by your goals

- You have a feeling that something is holding you back, but you're not sure what it is

Take Action
What's Sapping your Energy?

Write your life categories each on a separate page in your B.A.L.A.N.C.E. Journal. You can use the eight categories listed on in this chapter, or you can use your own, something that's more personal to you. Find a quiet space and think about each area. Ask yourself: What is draining my energy in this life area? What is causing conflict? What worries me? What keeps me up at night? What gets on my nerves? As you contemplate all your life categories, consider your energy sappers, including tolerations and incompletes.

<u>Tolerations</u> are irritants, inconveniences, aggravations, and annoyances that you barely even notice are sapping your energy. You tolerate them, either because you don't feel like dealing with them or you don't even realize they're bothering you. Some examples include a leaky faucet, the 1980s wallpaper in your dining room, the mess in your refrigerator, chronic heartburn, and the piles of junk on your basement stairs. When most women really start to think about it, they find tons of tolerations in their lives. The good news is that most tolerations can be improved or eliminated — you just have to look around, notice them, and brainstorm ways to get in control of them. Your energy will surge when you tear down that awful wallpaper and put on a fresh coat of paint, perform a kamikaze cleanup on your refrigerator, or see your doctor for advice on reducing or eliminating your heart- burn. Freeing up that energy will give you more space to focus on achieving your most important goals.

<u>Incompletes</u> are energy sappers that result from unfinished business tugging at your mind. Examples include an insurance form that you filled in but never submitted, an overdue mammogram, a friend you no longer speak to but think about often, and a thank-you note that's three months overdue. As with tolerations, you can stop the energy drain that incompletes cause by identifying them and brainstorming ways to complete them so you can then push them out of your mind.

During my search for balance, I began taking classes to understand it better. What I learned validated my own experience, and I was

Chapter Seven - C is for Confront and Connect

now given some tools so I could help people better. I learned about the importance of looking at your whole life, your energy sappers, and your incompletes and tolerations from Stephen Cluney, a master coach and teacher at New York University. This has had a profound effect on me personally, and on many of the women I worked with.

When I started to identify and eliminate my tolerations and incompletes, I felt as if I transformed from a sponge to a powerful person— instead of allowing the negative energy around me to soak into me, it started to bounce off of me. I began to have more energy to take control of what I could control and change it for the better. Once you start identifying your energy sappers, you will feel lighter than ever.

As you list your various energy sappers, remember not to judge them, worry about them, or feel overwhelmed by them. By simply getting them down on paper, you're starting to confront them.

Just becoming aware of your energy sappers and articulating them will bring them to the forefront of your mind. This is an amazing process. Just recognizing energy sappers can begin the process of eliminating, fixing, or resolving them. If that happens, go with it. But if it doesn't, that's fine. Don't get stuck on them. For now, getting them down on paper is great.

Once you get all your energy sappers out of your head and into your notebook, it is as if one of the cluttered blackboards in your brain has been erased. With a clean slate, you're ready to move forward.

Be aware that there is a delicate balance between confronting issues and creating problems for yourself. If you focus on small issues, you can magnify them and make the obstacle bigger and bigger. Rather, we are confronting obstacles to create opportunities for change and forward movement.

Finally, keep this great quote in mind:

> *I've missed more than nine thousand shots in my career. I've lost almost three hundred games. Twenty-six times I've been trusted to take the game-winning shot and missed. I've failed over and over and over again in my life. And that is why I succeed.*
> —Michael Jordan

Here are six tips to help you handle the challenges that come along as you journey toward balance:

1. **Use your gut as your guide.** Often we look to someone or something external to guide us through life's bigger challenges. Tap in to your own power, and use your gut (not your head) as your guide. Sure, you can use your knowledge, but try not to overthink or overanalyze anything. Your gut is an amazing guide.

2. **Turn to your support team.** Reach out to your supporters as you confront your obstacles. Your support team may have Advice or may help you open your mind to strategies that may work for you. Even when your supporters don't have answers, they can listen. You know what real support means—you de- fined it in Chapter 5.

3. **Flip your focus.** It's normal to focus on problems, but it's not very helpful. Instead, try to flip your focus to what you can control and what you can do for yourself or others. If you know of a family in need of food, for example, make a meal, dessert, or gift basket for them. And if you don't have time to cook the meal, make a basket with all the ingredients. This will help take the focus off the stress in your life and fill you with good spirit.

4. **Stop trying to solve the problem.** When you focus really hard on solving a problem, you magnify it to the point that it's all you can think about. Paradoxically, sometimes the more you think about a problem, the harder it is to solve. Instead of fixating on what's wrong, shift your focus to all the good things going on in your life. For example, if you feel desperate to find a new job, try to put aside thoughts about coworkers and resumes and interviews, and instead delve into something completely different and wonderful—reconnecting with friends, doing a favorite activity, volunteering to help others, and using your unique gifts to make a difference in the world. When you get totally wrapped up in living your life, your problems often take care of themselves.

5. **Let your vision propel you forward.** When no clear answer is presenting itself, go back to basics—your vision, your faith, and your core values. Think about your vision for your life, and let God guide you. If you lose your job, you can react by frantically applying for every job under the sun, whether you're really interested in it or not. Or you can spend some time really thinking about your vision for a happy, satisfied life. What are you doing in that vision? How are you spending your days? Once you have a really good sense of your vision, it will help guide your next steps in a calm, mindful way.

6. **Believe that somehow this will teach you something.** Almost every problem, difficulty, and negative experience has hidden lessons that help you benefit and grow—eventually. Believing that there's a lesson in every challenge helps make the challenge a bit easier to bear. Go back to other tough times in your life and look at the lessons you gained from them. Then, have faith that you will someday learn from what you're coping with today. Trust that no matter how hard a problem is, you will grow from having faced it.

Handling an Unexpected Twist

I love the whole process of putting up our Christmas tree—pulling out the ornaments we've collected over the years, watching the kids jumping around us, fighting over who gets to hang the decorations and where things should go. Putting up the tree itself takes about ten minutes. There are three parts that snap together, and the white lights are pre-strung. So that's the simple part—usually. A couple years ago, our basement flooded, and when we put the tree together the following Christ- mas, we realized none of the lights worked. Michael tried every- thing, but there was no saving the lights. The wiring was all rotted from the inside.

Back in the basement, my hubby found a set of colored lights and did a quick wrap-around to see if we liked them. Of course, lulu and the Little Man were all in favor of colored lights! Lu said, "Mommy, those lights are WAAAAAYYYYY better than the other ones we had last year!" The lights did have a magic to them—they were a little larger and had a nice glow.

So, the hubby said, "What do we do? Do I just string them over the top? The old lights are strung between every branch." My little smile made my husband cringe—he knew this quick fix wasn't the answer. Stringing the bright, hopeful colored lights over the broken ones didn't sit well with me. We needed to take the tree apart, remove the old lights, and replace them with new ones. Michael didn't love this idea. He even offered to run to Home Depot for another tree. But we both knew that wasn't the answer, as this tree was barely four years old. So, branch by knotted branch, we carefully removed every single light.

Lu and the Little Man cheered us on. They couldn't wait to hang the ornaments. The anticipation was priceless. Still, it was definitely an exercise in patience. I silently repeated a word that helps me in situations like this: aretae, which means "patience is a virtue." When my husband would breathe an extra-loud huff, I reminded him how beautiful the tree would look when we finished. As we worked, I pondered the message that the tree was giving us: a message of authenticity, change, hard work, patience, and ultimately, after almost four hours spent removing the lights, appreciation.

The tree decorating lasted throughout the day. When we finished, we took a step back in awe of the beautiful tree that had almost made us rip our hair out. Michael and I agreed it was so worth it.

Coping with Common Obstacles

We have to embrace obstacles to reach the next stage of joy.
—Goldie Hawn

By understanding the obstacles that can tangle you on your balance journey, you can prepare yourself and be ready when they come your way. Here are some of the most common obstacles as well as tips on confronting them.

Obstacle: Expensive Food
Take charge: When you're trying to fuel your body well, money can sometimes be an obstacle. Here are some things you can do to over- come it:
• coupons for fresh food aren't often readily available, but you can find them online. Google the exact foods you'd like to buy (i.e., coupons fresh strawberries) and you will find discounts and coupons that will help lower the cost.
• Go frozen or canned to save big time. Frozen veggies such as spinach or broccoli and fruits such as strawberries and blueberries are way cheaper than fresh produce. Many are frozen or canned immediately after harvesting, so they have the same nutritional value as fresh produce. When buying canned or

Chapter Seven - C is for Confront and Connect

frozen fruits or vegetables, be sure to choose those without any added sugar or salt.

• Stock up on sale foods. When produce is on sale, buy extra and freeze it.

• Go beyond the supermarket. Look for bargains at farmers markets, alternative grocers such as Trader Joe's, food co-ops, community gardens, and local farm stands.

• Make a grocery list with your budget in mind, and stick to it. The extras that we toss in the shopping cart really add up!

• Make beans a staple in your diet. Kidney beans, black beans, white beans, pinto beans, baked beans—they're full of vitamins and fiber and are cheap, cheap, cheap. Buy them in cans or save even more money choosing dried beans that you cook up yourself.

Obstacle: Fear of Change
Take charge: We often refer to 'change' as taking a leap of faith. I use that phrase myself sometimes! But, jumping off anything is scary for most people. Can you imagine going to the edge of a cliff, with no safety gear at all, and just jumping off of it?! Of course not, or at least, I hope not!! Walking down the street is not nearly as frightening.

I've spoken to so many people about their hopes and dreams, but fear keeps them at status quo. I get it - they consider their dream similar to being at the edge of cliff and taking a "leap" off can be daunting.

Once I heard Pastor Joe Gratzel talking about this, and his words went straight to my heart and stayed there for whenever I feel my own fears. He said, "It's not really a "leap of faith" if you have faith. It's actually just a walk in faith."

So, when fear begins to hold you back from your pure potential {in any aspect of your being}, just visualize yourself walking down the street in faith. And, if your heart feels like leaping, just because leaping can be exhilarating, remember your faith is the safety gear and you are not alone.

Obstacle: A Crowded Mind
Take charge: Meditate, even for a minute. Prayer is speaking to God, and meditation is listening. Your innate wisdom has so much to tell you, but you won't hear it unless you shut everything else

out and listen. Even a minute of meditation goes a long way—certainly you can find a minute here and there to clear your mind. Close your eyes, breathe deeply, and let go of your fears. A clear mind helps us kick out the junk and connect with our purpose, so picture a white light and focus.

Obstacle: Unsupportive People
Take charge: it's frustrating when the people around you are not in line with your goals. When this happens, you usually can't change others, but you can control what you do, how you react, and your own actions. Focus on what you can do to move forward and still be the best version of yourself possible. Don't give other people's negative behaviors any more power in your life—try to focus only on the things you can control. Remember that nothing others do or say is because of us, and you have no idea what could possibly be going on beyond the surface of their lives. They may be dealing with challenging personal struggles, and not being supportive of others is just a symptom of something much deeper for them. Love them just the same, and don't let them weigh you down.

Obstacle: Hurtful Comments
A journalist once asked me if I had ever received hurtful comments from strangers about my weight. My answer was, "Who hasn't?" People had commented on my weight and size for as long as I can remember. In grammar school, when I was the tallest kid in the class, my nickname was Big T. Once, when I was grocery shopping, a little boy asked me if he could rub my belly. His mother just laughed and said, "Never mind him. He thinks you're pregnant." We've all had someone, most often unintentionally, say something hurtful.
Take charge: Remember that everything a person says or does is a reflection of his or her own inner state. Learn to love and accept yourself, and know your strength comes from God. You're your heart on to people who make hurtful comments by showing compassion to where they are in their own life journey.

Here are some things I learned about dealing with comments from people:

• Practice self-care. Love and nurture yourself no matter what others say. Nourish your body, mind, and spirit while practicing self-care. Don't allow degrading comments to diminish your light.
• Don't fire back—inquire. Being curious is always a good thing. Asking questions opens up your mind to what others are thinking. When people say something that doesn't feel right or kind

to you, ask them about it. Don't be defensive or assume they mean the worst. Try simple questions, like, "What do you mean by that?" Or "Why do you ask?" This allows them to explain what they actually mean—and if they spoke carelessly, to realize how hurtful comments can be. I'm sure we've all put our feet in our mouths at some point and would have loved the opportunity to explain, so give others that opportunity.

• Realize that sometimes it's just your interpretation. Haven't you ever read into something and realized later you were completely wrong? When our self-esteem is low, or we're having a bad day, we tend to look for negative comments and assume everything is meant to hurt us. I distinctly remember being in the gym locker room watching girls laugh and totally assuming they were laughing at me. I felt awful all day, until I later learned they were laughing at a comment scratched into the locker! Remember, if you look for negativity, you will always find it, even if it doesn't truly exist.

• Be kind. It can feel difficult not to immediately get offended or hurt. But by staying strong, you won't allow other people's stress or negativity into your heart. Open up to the human being—they have their own story that may explain their behavior. Be compassionate. Instead of being defensive, you'll feel positive energy inside you. Energy is contagious, so why not pass along your positive energy? Kindness inspires people.

Tart but Sweet

Years ago, whenever I had a problem, I would stew on it forever. I'd call up every one of my friends, ask for advice, vent, circle back and forth, and seesaw up and down trying to figure out the answers. The problem would take hostage of my brain, and it was all I could think about until there was some sort of resolution or so much time had passed that the problem faded into the background of my mind.

I can't imagine how many hours I wasted. I was so wrapped up in my own world—it was just a tangled mess. As I got a little older, and the problems got a little tougher, somewhere, somehow over the last decade, I learned a profound lesson:

When life hands you lemons, make someone else lemonade.

Whether it's volunteering, helping a friend organize her office, or paying for a stranger's cup of coffee— just connecting with the world around me in a positive way can almost immediately lift my spirit. Honestly, I can't remember exactly when or how this dawned on me, but truly when I realized I should step outside of myself, help others, and stop wasting time on empty worrying, my whole world changed. And just by virtue of experience, it became a lesson.

The sun seemed a bit brighter. The clouds became more beautiful. The rain, which once symbolized despair, turned into a blessing, a cleansing, soulful dance. Of course, I am human. And there are times when I have to vent with tears or talking, but where I once took forever to get over problems, now it takes just moments.

And although I am writing about it, the proof is in the action. This is something that words really can't teach and money can't buy. We find ourselves in other people; we find our unique gifts when we have nothing else left but those to use.

B.A.L.A.N.C.E. Technique #12 :
Connecting with Humanity and All of God's Creation

Stressful moments have a way of popping up when you least expect them. But having a list of tried-and-true simple, soulful B.A.L.A.N.C.E. Techniques can help you push away the frazzles and feel better quickly. One of my favorites is connecting.

Sharing a moment of connection with another living being can tame your temper, pull down your defenses, distract you from your troubles, and replace distress with deep appreciation for life.

The connection can take many forms. You can connect with a family member, a friend, a coworker, a member of your support team, a mentor, a neighbor, or a complete stranger. You can have a go-to connection such as your best friend or your spouse, or you can pick someone different depending on what's stressing you out. Discussing your troubles with someone who's been down the same path can be very encouraging.

Even an empathetic stranger can provide that pick-me-up human connection that warms your heart. Alice found her blood boiling at a large discount store's self-checkout line when she realized the customer in front of her was paying for a large order with dollar bills that had to be fed into the cash collector one at a time. After several minutes spent watching the woman fumble tediously with crumpled bills and wondering why she didn't pick the full-serve line, Alice glanced at another customer who rolled her eyes and smiled. That simple empathetic connection turned the moment from frustrating to silly, and she was able to relax and appreciate the goofiness of the situation rather than get steamed up with stress. And after all, everyone has a story, and the woman with the crumpled bills is no exception.

I know I created a little stress myself - I went to Staples to get supplies for my Challenge class, and when I was paying at the register, I noticed an adorable reusable shopping bag at the counter next to mine. I asked the woman ringing me up if I could grab it, and she said, "Of course!" But, from behind I heard many loud sighs of annoyance. I smiled at the short line and apologized, it only took me a second to grab the bag, but yet I could tell that it upset some customers waiting. I realized in that moment how fast-paced our world has become, and made a conscious note not to allow seconds to cause stress or sighing.

However, my smile caught the eye of the woman behind me, and she giggled at herself for being upset! We had a casual (and quick) exchange, and I left the store uplifted by the connection!

Connecting doesn't have to mean spending a lot of time with another person, although that's great if you can manage it. Even a quick phone call or a brief chat can make a big difference.

Connect with a Furry or Feathered Friend

You can also connect with a pet. Anyone who owns a beloved dog or cat knows how comforting it can be to spend time together walking, playing, petting, or just sitting.

Our family dog Stella and our little blue birdie Echo bring so much joy into our home - they are pure, unconditional love! I love listening to the birdie sing, and the kiddos often play music for him, Lulu lets him perch on her finger, and little man talks to him.

Dogs in particular can lend such a calming presence that they're sometimes paired up with children undergoing scary tests in hospitals and with lonely nursing home residents. Studies show that petting a dog can lower blood pressure, improve mood, and generate feelings of well-being. I'm sure a purring cat can have the same effect when curled up on someone's lap - unfortunately I'm allergic to cats!!

When you connect an animal, you're reminded of the fact that you're not alone in the world. You're reminded that you are worthy of love, unconditionally. It helps put your stressors in perspective.

Connect in Your Community

In this very busy, fast-paced, plugged-in world, it's easy to get caught up in the hustle and bustle of life and forget the incredible gift of connecting off-line and right in our communities.

As a child, joining a club happens regularly—I remember being a Girl Scout and being in the chorus. We even had a club in high school for poets and writers. As an adult, joining a club may seem frivolous at first, but on the contrary, being a part of a club, organization, or community often enriches our lives and fills our spiritual tanks.

Joining a community is amazing for so many reasons: sharing interests, such as scrapbooking, swimming, writing, or reading great books; having a supportive group of people who share your goals, hopes, faith, and dreams; and working together for a greater good in volunteering, reaching out, or sharing your gifts with the world. And sometimes being part of a group is exactly what we need to just play, let loose, have fun, and tap in to our inner child. So give yourself permission to just go with it and get involved.

Here are some examples of simple acts of kindness that we can do that allow our hearts to connect with people in our community:

* Bring a small token such as an ornament or packet of seeds to your "regulars" (i.e. the cashier at Dunkin' Donuts, your bank teller)

* Be a blessing anonymously to a family struggling to put food on the table - put together a basket filled with items to make a full dinner (and all the supplies needed to make the dinner). Let the presentation speak your love, with the time, attention, and details you put into making it. Handwrite your family's favorite recipe on a card.

* Purchase something to donate any chance you get- buy an extra canned good, an extra toy, an extra towel, or pair of slippers. You can also think beyond basic needs and donate something that touches the heart as well - a token with an inspirational message

or something handmade.

* Bring your spare change and give it to the person at the Coin Star machine or Salvation Army stands.

* Write out Gratitude Cards with a special message to leave anonymously behind at counters, in changing rooms, at checkout lines

* Bring little bits of sweetness with you and wrap inspirational messages around them to hand out to people waiting on line, or just leave them on the counter or in fitting rooms. A small piece of dark chocolate that says "You are magnificent..." may be just the pick me up a stranger needs that will lift your spirits as well!

And most of all, remember to always be patient with yourself and others, be gentle. We do not know what others are going through- life can be difficult for us all at times. Smiles are healing, and we never know the effect we have on each other!!

Connect by Offering Forgiveness

The practice of forgiveness is our most important contribution to the healing of the world. - Marianne Williamson

I think everyone has had relationships (from friendship to family to romantic to work) that have left them feeling broken or feeling a bit 'incomplete', because for whatever reason the relationship changed or ended abruptly or slowly over time you lost touch.

Situations happen, from hurtful comments to misunderstandings to errors in judgment to personalities clashing - these things can easily make for difficult relationships.

I think it's fairly common to 'surface forgive' in order to smooth it over. But, when we 'surface forgive', we actually are still holding on to resentment and uneasy feelings on the inside. Surface forgiving is like stuffing down the hurt to block our vocal chords from speaking. And, when we 'surface forgive', we choose to just carry on, either by ending the relationship swiftly or by continuing it as if nothing happened. This wreaks havoc on our health and does no good in healing relationships, it may even deepen the wedge.

I know the old saying 'forgive and forget', but can we ever really do it without the practice of true forgiveness?

True forgiveness isn't about just getting along, and doesn't have to be about dumping the relationship entirely. It's not about right or wrong. It's about understanding that we are each imperfect, that we may not always see eye to eye, that miscommunications are a 2-way street. Practicing true forgiveness connects us as human beings- each of us is flawed, yet beautiful in our own ways. We all put our foot in our mouth, don't always say or do the 'right' things, make mistakes. I believe most people have good intent, but delivery or content may not always be 'perfect'. It's about understanding that people are affected by stress differently, and if they are going through difficult times, choosing to be compassionate, not defensive will change your perspective entirely.

True forgiveness is about recognizing that we all have a history that impacts our actions, and often our thoughts, and that there may be deep reasons another human being "is" the way he or she is, and none of us are exempt from making mistakes. Instead, let go of the anger or frustration.

Let me be clear, I don't think true forgiveness means we have to accept standards of behavior that are less than we deserve. If your gut is telling you something is unacceptable, you should remove yourself from the situation or release yourself from the relationship. And make peace with it, forgive, and move forward in your life.

True forgiveness sets us free, lightens the load that drags us down. So, today choose to practice forgiveness...release the uncomfortable feeling of discord, and instead listen with compassion, communicate with your heart, be gentler on both yourself and others.

What does forgiveness mean to you? How do you practice true forgiveness in your life?

Where Do We Find Connection?

I was teaching a class recently and when the topic of "connecting with each other" came up, a woman laughed out loud. She even rolled her eyes at me and said the "days of loving our neighbor as ourselves are over."

A bit deflated by her response at first, I understood, and her reaction was not unique - I felt people question this topic before and sometimes I even joke about it to point out the proverbial "elephant in the room" whether anyone says anything openly or not. I was grateful for this woman challenging my words because this began a conversation about what "connecting" actually means, and we connected even more.

The woman said many people annoyed her, and are selfish, which in turn hardened her heart and made her selfish back. She wasn't even sure if she believed in love period. She said with little exception, "love" was nowhere to be found, at least not in the places she frequented - at the office, in the food store, the post office, the bank, even in her place of worship - people seemed disconnected and in a rush, annoyed at everything. Again, all things I've heard (and even felt) myself before.

But, I do believe the lens in which we view the world from transforms our experience of this precious gift called life. What we seek, we always find {Matthew 7:7}. Was the woman in the class really looking for love or was she secretly expecting a let down? She confessed she had low expectations of people based on prior experiences.

So where do we seek? Where is love?

I remember the first time I saw the play "Oliver". I adored the young actor who played Oliver, and his sweet, soft voice singing "Where is Love?" literally made this little girl stream tears. He sang, "Where is love? Does it fall from skies above? Is it underneath the willow tree that I've been dreaming of?"

And with that, I began to bawl. I didn't quite understand why at the time - there I was, just a child really, and feeling such incredible emotions. Now I get that it is in others that we see ourselves, that every emotion is just a reflection of our own humanity, and it is in that connection that we find the answer to Oliver's question of "where is love?" Love is within us all, because God is love.

Love is present, love is real - whether you believe in love or God or not, He is with us. Kind of like oxygen, no I can't see it, but I trust it's there because I'm breathing, and I trust we all have access to it because we are all alive as long as we don't hold back our breath. But when a person experiences atrophy of the lungs and the lungs stiffen, it makes it near impossible to breathe. I thought about the woman in my class with her hardened heart, and wondered if when our hearts stiffen up, does it makes it near impossible to love?

Love, like oxygen, is universal, we all have access to it, as long as we don't hold back - everyone who has a heart that beats knows love when they experience it...I felt love one day when the man pumping gas (who didn't speak much English) looked at my little man and his eyes filled with tears. He grabbed his wallet to show me a picture of his daughter and said "2 years until she's here." If we only knew each others' hearts - we are all the same...

I equate love with God, as I believe they are one in the same. At one time, I thought God was just in all things positive. I believed that God was in the good, and, while God is "light", that assumption was technically not true - God was in Oliver's sadness as he sang. God was in my tears as I felt the words sting my young, precious heart. God was in the gas attendant's trembling hand as he showed me the picture of his daughter.

God is in everything, every smile, every heartache, every love story, every disappointment, every dream come true, every prayer answered or not - God is in the cracks, the stains, the imperfections, the commotion, the darkness. He is in the beauty, the laughter, the stillness, the light. He is with us through it all, and while some of us display God's light through strength, others are the embodiment of God's amazing grace in our weaknesses.

It is all His miraculous presence enveloping us. When I seek Him, I see God in the anger, in the fear. I see God in the wretched, in the woman on her knees asking for forgiveness. I see God in the baby fast asleep and the beggar on the street. I see God in you and me and in every part of humanity, it's God - that's all I see.

I am in love with the beautiful messes we all are, the cracked fragmented beings walking this earth, every one of us - and I am in awe of His mercy, knowing God loves us through joy and pain, {whether we are on top of the mountain or down in the valley or anywhere in between} and asks us to come as we are. And when we do, when we seek Him, hardened hearts heal, we are transformed, and we find the love we are looking for. And that is the most beautiful connection we can find.

Chapter Seven - C is for Confront and Connect

Summing up

In this chapter, we discussed the importance of confronting obstacles and root issues:

- How to identify obstacles
- How to use the over-through-around technique
- The importance of finding your UHOs
- Understanding the circles of life and how they affect each other if minor issues are not addressed
- Brainstorming ways to surmount your obstacles
- Confronting problems at the root to peacefully resolve them
- The value of connecting with others to reduce stress and generate calmness

In the next chapter, we'll talk about engaging —committing completely to changing your life for the better, living passionately, and learning from failure.

Chapter Eight
E is for Engage and Experience

You cannot help but learn more as you take the world into your hands. Take it up reverently, for it is an old piece of clay, with millions of thumbprints on it.
—John Updike

My husband and I feel as if Lulu and Little Man have been in our lives forever. We can hardly remember a time without them, and we are blessed to have them in our world. We have learned so much from them in the past eleven years. They are the loves of our lives.

Looking at the world through their eyes has been an incredible gift. It's allowed us to see some of the moments that we adults often miss. Using a child's perspective can allow us to engage in the world around us in a way that allows our hearts to open up and more fully experience the gift of life.

We are born in awe, constantly amazed at the world, inspired by nature, and fearless. It's a beautiful way to live, and unfortunately it's a perspective many people lose over the years. Imagine regaining that childlike point of view and reconnecting with that part of yourself. It sounds impossible, but it's not. We really can add that essence back into our grown-up life view.
Seeing the world in an awe-filled, inspired, fearless way—engaging

Chapter Eight - E is for Engage and Experience

fully and completely in the world around you—is the topic of the last of the B.A.L.A.N.C.E. Techniques. In this chapter, we'll focus on engaging.

You've come so far since the beginning of the book. You learned to clear your mind and listen to your heart. You've let go of the baggage that has held you down and added in choices and behaviors that will help you feel balanced and whole. You created a renewed life vision, learned to set goals, and gathered a set of tools that will allow you to navigate your journey and confront obstacles that pop up along the way. Now it's time to engage yourself fully in the life you envisioned by making a complete commitment to incorporating everything you've learned and discovered into your life. You've learned all the tools and techniques—now it's time to pull everything together and engage in a life of energy, passion, excitement, and joy.

By now you know that I can't tell you exactly how to do this. The power to engage passionately in life has to come from deep within your soul. You are divine being, and you have everything you need right inside of you, because God will never leave you.

B.AL.A.N.C.E Technique #13
Engage: In This Miraculous Gift of Life

My mission in life is not merely to survive, but to thrive; and to do so with some passion, some compassion, some humor, and some style. —Maya Angelou

What does engaging in your life mean to you? Here's what it means to me:

Whatever you do, commit to it completely. Once you make a choice that aligns with your vision and your core values, embrace it 100 percent. Celebrate it. Enjoy it. Love it. Whether it's a small choice (which soap to buy), a food choice (which breakfast to eat), or a major life decision (which career path to follow), embrace it with energy and passion. Even if it's a choice that doesn't align completely with your goals, love it anyhow If you have a homemade fudgy brownie with your lunch, don't feel guilty about it— enjoy every bite. Savor the flavor, the rich, chocolate goodness. If you're going to eat it, love it!

Plug in to each moment. Engaging in life means plugging in,

feeling it, living it, being fully and completely awakened. Open your eyes wider and engage in the world around you. Right now, feel the paper of this book you are reading (or the case of the electronic reader, if you've downloaded it), and feel the firmness of your feet on the ground (or the softness of the couch you're cuddled up on). Notice the temperature of the room, the light pouring in the window, the taste of the water with lemon in the glass by your side, the scent of the herb-encrusted chicken you've got roasting in the oven. (okay, you may not be roasting a chicken, but we can dream, can't we?)

Use all of your senses.

The same goes for your emotions. Plug in to them, feel them, let them flow, and respond to them. If you are tired, plug in to rest. Allow yourself the comfort of closing your eyes, leaving your cell phone out of your bedroom, and allowing yourself to plug in—fully and without guilt—to sleep. (By the way, I know women who choose to remove all electronics from their bedroom, and they swear they sleep more soundly.)

Say good-bye to guilt. Nobody is perfect, and if God gives us grace and mercy, we can certainly give it to ourselves, too. We all stray from our vision sometimes and make choices that don't line up. We are human; we don't always say or do the right thing. When that happens, don't get stuck in a cloud of guilt. Turn it into a positive experience by learning its lesson. Realize that your choices should make you feel alive and excited, not down and defeated. If you make a choice that isn't honoring who you are, learn from it and then move forward making the next choice a more soul-centered one. Everything that teaches us more about ourselves or this gift of life is a positive thing, so absorb its lesson and move on.

Relish the simple joys of life. Let's face it—most days are pretty routine. You get up, work, do some laundry, make dinner, put your kids to bed. But if you are fully, passionately engaged in life, it's so much easier to relish the simple joys that come along so many times every day. When you're engaged, there can be joy in every detail, in even the most mundane tasks. Notice it, appreciate it, and celebrate it!

Embrace the notion of motion. Aim to live in motion rather than just existing and going through the motions of life. Being in motion doesn't mean to go-go-go at a frantic pace—do that, and you'll miss some of the best moments. It means being fully invested in every moment of the day. Whatever you do, do it with passion. Breathe in the morning air. Sing in the car. Converse deeply about everyday occurrences with your family, neighbors, and friends.

Make a breakfast in bed for your spouse or loved ones. Give yourself a foot massage, or go get one (be sure to turn your cell phone off). Write in a journal, frame your favorite photos, sit in your car and enjoy a sunset, write a thank-you note to your favorite childhood friend or teacher. Do what makes your soul stir so you can live well with passion and energy!

Learn from failure. How many times have you tried something and not succeeded? Believe me, I am a living testament to the motto: if at first you don't succeed, try, try again! The beautiful thing about failure is that it has so much to teach. Turning failure into opportunity can be hard, so here are three tips that can help:

1. Look back for understanding. When you fail, you want to crawl in a hole and forget about it. But you can't move forward if you're cowering in a hole. Evaluate what happened—the good and the bad. Be honest with yourself. What was the lesson? What was the gift in the imperfection?

2. Ask for feedback. Sometimes you can't define or face the reasons for your failure. When that happens, ask a supporter to help you confront the truth, look at the whole picture, and learn valuable lessons.

3. Go back to the source. Sometimes we fail because we're chasing a goal that doesn't really line up with our vision and core values. When failure strikes, reevaluate your goals and values and listen to your heart. You may discover the failure was a blessing in disguise and that you really should be following a different path.

As we drive along this road called life, occasionally a gal will find herself a little lost. And when that happens, I guess she has to let go of the "coulda, shoulda, woulda," buckle up and just keep going.
—Carrie Bradshaw, Sex and the City

Appreciate simplicity. There are times when nothing is happening. Instead of feeling bored and disappointed, engage with the moment and appreciate all the beauty in the peacefulness. Take a deep, clear breath and relish the fact that you are alive. When you are walking down the street, appreciate that your legs work. Smell a flower and savor the fact that your nose is so beautifully designed that it can extract joyful scents from something you pull out of the ground. Live every minute. Time going quickly is not a misconception. Don't blink—your life can pass you by if you don't really live it. Embrace life, and live it! Do the things you love to do and you will attract new people and experiences into your world. If you love nature, find places to go for hikes, spend some time outdoors every day, and appreciate nature wherever you see it, even if it's just in glimpses from the window of your car. If you are a writer, buy a journal, grab a pen, and start writing. Engage in life, make the most of every experience you have, even the simplest of moments.

Work hard but always make time to listen to the music. I learned this lesson from an amazing woman named Mary Lou. You may have noticed she was one of the 'original inspiristas' this book is dedicated to. My Little Man and LuLu called her 'Miss Mary Lou' which always melted my heart, so that's how I think of her, as Miss Mary Lou.

I have notebooks filled with thoughts after every conversation I had with her. She was a fierce business woman, no-nonsense, straight forward friend, paired with the heart of an angel, and a childlike spirit. The juxtaposition of these characteristics was endearing and inspiring. She was a mentor, she was family.

She worked hard, loved entrepreneurs, ideas, innovation, business. She also loved music, art, nature, food, laughter, fun. I will never forget the times she would show up with something musical, like Mickey Mouse characters that played Christmas songs or the Teddy Bear that played the piano - we all would watch in awe, and no matter how many times they played, she still had wonder in her eyes. Her smile touched every heart it met.

She always believed in me. No matter what I was doing, she encouraged me. She listened without judgement. She shared her own personal stories. She lifted me up no matter how much of a mess I felt like or how many mistakes I might have made. She never allowed me to question my worth. And then, she let me have the truth. She gave advice, offered solutions, and guided me. Last Spring, she went to be with the Lord. I will miss our conversations. I will miss having her to call. I will miss her stories. I will miss her. Until we meet again, dear friend.

Chapter Eight - E is for Engage and Experience

The most difficult thing is the decision to act,
The rest is merely tenacity. The fears are paper tigers.
You can do anything you decide to do.
—Amelia Earhart

My husband surprised me with a new bike. It had been over fifteen years since I'd actually owned a bike, and I have to admit, although I really did want to ride, I was pretty scared. Would I fall off? Would I be able to brake? Turn? Avoid parked cars? Veer out into traffic? Would I be able to go downhill? Uphill?

I took a few minutes to introduce myself to the bike and rode it gingerly up and down my block on the sidewalk. My neighbor saw me and smiled. I felt like I was eight years old again, on my bike for the very first time—cautious, slow, using my feet to slow down.

The next morning I woke up ready to really face my fears and ride that bike on the road. Little Man had just woken up, Michael was drinking his morning coffee, and lulu was still asleep. "I'll be right back, hon. I'm just going to ride up and down the street for five minutes. I want to get my bearings."

My husband laughed. Just the day before, he'd ridden by the beach for almost two hours. "Okay, babe," he said. "Have fun!"

I rode onto the street—it wasn't so bad. I picked up speed, and it felt kind of exhilarating. Then I biked around my neighborhood, the wind in my hair, the sun on my face. "Woo-hoo!" I actually shouted out loud. A lady walking her dog laughed, and I waved—with one hand off the handlebars!

A few blocks away from us, homes are set on the water. It's beautiful and serene, with very little traffic. I biked up and down, back and forth, smiling the entire time. It was over forty minutes, and I could have gone longer, but Lulu would be waking up soon and I wanted to give her a good morning kiss.

I walked in the door singing. How happy I was to have faced my fear!

What will you do today to face a fear?

Zen Quickies
Ten Ways to Engage Instantly in Life
1. Play a game from your childhood—checkers, Scrabble, Operation, Twister.
2. Sing in your shower, car, yard, or office.
3. Have a good laugh.
4. Apologize—don't let bad feelings linger.
5. Accept an apology.
6. Have a good cry.
7. Take the day off and lounge in sweats all day.
8. Get dressed to the nines for no reason.
9. Walk a neighbor's dog.
10. Cash in all of your spare change and give it to someone who could use a little help.

Engage in What You Set out to Do:
Your 30-Day challenge

Over the course of thirty days, I challenge them to make changes so they can align their thoughts with their actions. Now I'm going to give you that same challenge: to commit fully to what you want and to engage wholeheartedly in what you're setting out to do.

Take action

What's your challenge?
Over the next thirty days, create a challenge for yourself. Push yourself outside of your comfort zone, try something new, enroll in a class, get involved in an activity, use your gifts, create new recipes, have some fun, light up a room, walk a little faster, or park a little farther away. Let your vision guide you, your core values be your compass, and remember, the possibilities are limitless.

You can choose a daily challenge, like some of these my clients have done:

• I got in touch with my younger self and started a jigsaw puzzle during the storm.
• I jumped rope for twenty-five minutes—I broke out into a sweat unlike I've felt in years!
• I walked three miles outdoors with some old friends.
• I packed all my meals for the week in Tupperware, and they look delicious.

Chapter Eight - E is for Engage and Experience

- I donated my time in a soup kitchen. It was much healthier and far more fulfilling than being home, bored, and eating on the couch.
- I made a video of myself talking about what I wanted for my life, and I am even contemplating starting a blog about it. Maybe that will be tomorrow's challenge, definitely out of my comfort zone!

Or it can be a monthly challenge:

- I registered for three cooking classes at a county college to think outside the box!
- I joined a support group for women whose husbands are overseas.
- I began bike riding again, and I am choosing to eat only fresh, natural foods.
- I chose to be more pleasant at work and nicer to my coworkers. Believe it or not, I actually began a midday walking group with five other women in the office.
- I dusted off my art supplies and am going to begin painting again. This will get me out of my after-work rut of chips and dip before dinner.
- I am training for a thirty-mile walk to raise money for breast cancer.

Now you've got some ideas. How will you challenge yourself to change this month? What actions can you take to engage in what you set out to do?

Making Engaging Effortless

Lately I've been really watching the birds fly, a lot. This morning I happened to catch a glimpse of one gliding just a few feet in front of me, and I marveled at the way it seemed effortless and carefree. Many people equate flying or soaring with success, but I think it's more than that; I also equate it with trust, faith, peace, and overcoming challenges.

When a bird flaps its wings, air is pushed down. This opposition in force lifts the bird in the air. It's not easy to oppose something. Baby birds have to trust that the flapping will take them in the air. They fall, they must get back into the air, and they fall again—they must have faith in themselves that they can fly. They must believe.

Once the bird hits the air, watching it fly is peaceful. I closed my eyes after I saw the bird this morning. I imagined the smooth feeling of flight, and I began to picture all the people that make difficult work seem effortless: A-rod hitting a home run, Fred Astaire and Ginger Rogers dancing, Carrie Underwood belting out high notes. Effortless. And this makes me think about life. Can life really be effortless?

Engaging in life may feel like it is going to take a lot of effort. You've already got a long to-do list, and now we are adding in challenges and new activities. I'm not going to lie— but most anything does, it's just choosing which work you'd like to spend your time on. And once you do the work, it becomes part of you.

Effortlessness does not mean without work or challenges. To me, living effortlessly means living with joy and lightness, releasing the weight on your shoulders, leaning on God's wisdom, working hard but with a purpose, and living with passion. Oh yes, life can be effortless.

How do you define effortless? When does your life feel effortless? What work will you do to create what you want for your life? What ways can you begin engaging in life? My life feels effortless when:

- I breathe deeply.

- I am fully in the moment, connected to the present.

- I trust completely that everything happens for a reason.

- I witness my kids' pure joy over the little things—bubbles in the backyard, the sound of a motorcycle or truck rattling down the road, and seeing the neighbor when she's out walking her dogs.

- I choose faith over fear.

- I am grateful—not just back-of-the-mind grateful but truly steeped in gratitude and appreciation.

- I communicate my thoughts clearly, and I listen openly to others.

- I include fun and play in my daily life.

- I clear my mental plate and simplify, simplify, simplify.

Chapter Eight - E is for Engage and Experience

- I turn the radio up loud and sing along with my favorite songs.
- I follow the flow of good energy.
- I step outside of myself and give to others.

B.A.L.A.N.C.E Technique #14:
Experience the Moment

How we spend our days, is, of course, how we spend our lives.
—Annie Dillard

The last B.A.L.A.N.C.E. Technique is all about creating an experience. When you're stressed, tired, harried, and just need a Zen Quickie, this final technique is amazing. It doesn't have to take long to have a profound impact on your mood and stress level. In just a few moments, with a bit of creativity, some imagination, and a sense of fun, you can bring about near-magical transformations.

Think about it: all you need is a little glue, some glitter, a few sequins, and a couple rhinestones to turn an old pair of shoes into a pair of ruby slippers that can take you anywhere.

Start looking for ways to infuse everyday experiences with joy and happiness. Here are some suggestions for simple transformations:
Turn a shower into a spa treatment. Pick a soap that smells fantastic, and really take note of the scent. Breathe deeply in the shower. Be present. Don't let your mind wander to your to-do list—enjoy it with all of your senses.

You can also use some of your favorite kitchen ingredients to make a homemade scrub or hair treatment. Create a milk and honey scrub by mixing 1/3 cup sea salt, 1 tablespoon milk, a squeeze of honey, and a drop of olive oil. If your hair needs some TLC, try this coconut hair treatment: add some coconut oil and a splash of coconut milk to your favorite conditioner. Or make your own conditioner by mixing coconut oil, coconut milk, an egg, and a teaspoon of honey.

Add meaning to your morning coffee. I love my morning coffee, so taking this ordinary activity to extraordinary is super-simple for me. I love using meaningful mugs. I'm not talking about fine china, but something that evokes a feeling or a memory—a dragonfly mug that reminds me of my grandmother, for example. And a mug decorated by my kids reminds me of how beautiful life is in a child's eyes. Be sure to switch it up so it doesn't become the same old mug.

Another way to make ordinary morning coffee an extraordinary experience is by creating simple versions of café-style coffee. Heat up some milk, froth it up with a whisk, add a dash of cinnamon, and turn your everyday coffee into café au lait. For a richer café-style blend, try a dark-roasted bean, such as French roast or Sumatra roast. Something rich in flavor will really jazz up your morning coffee. Having a few varieties of coffee on hand is a good way to keep it interesting—dark roast one day, hazelnut the next, and Colombian the following day.

Add pleasure to every encounter. We see people all the time—in the neighborhood, while walking the dog, and at school, the bank, toll booths, and stores. Instead of giving a nod or a wave, make every connection extraordinary. Smile, say hello, stop and chat. Smile with your eyes and be genuinely happy to see others. If you spread happiness to them, and they spread happiness to the next person they see, an ordinary activity can become a chain of joy.

Brighten someone's day. Recently, a complete stranger made my day. While I was at the convenience store, the woman in line beside me gave me a huge grin and said she liked my shoes! I immediately smiled back and complimented her on her handbag. These are little things, but they made us both smile. It made me think about how many simple ways there are for us to do something nice for each other. Here are just a few:

- at work, stick a note to someone's computer: Great presentation at the meeting yesterday. Or, Thanks for always being there. Or, Love the necklace!

- Give someone a sincere, unexpected compliment.

- Ask to see photos of someone's kids, new boyfriend, family, vacation, home, or whatever it is they love.

- Send a handwritten note for no reason at all to your spouse, children, mom, or best friend. Because they see you regularly, they will be extra surprised by this simple gesture!

- follow up on previous conversations. Ask your colleague how her son is doing in his new college, whether your neighbor's new granddaughter has a new tooth, how your hairdresser's mother is feeling after her hip replacement surgery. People like to share, but sometimes they feel it's boring or selfish to talk about themselves unless they are asked. Remembering and asking about what's going on in people's lives can really brighten their day.

- Take off the shades, turn off the cell phone, and make eye contact with strangers.

- Give a small gift to someone who's been feeling down. Bake cookies, buy a bar of scented soap, or pick up a candle or a picture frame at a discount store. Wrap it in pretty tissue with a bow, enclose a short note, and let the person know you're thinking of her and are there for her if she needs help.

- Write a love letter. There's something about writing out our feelings that is inspiring, cathartic, and connects us on a deeper level. Take a few minutes to write a love letter to anyone—your partner, your best friend, your mom, your dad, your children, your first influential school teacher, your neighbor who waters your plants, or your postal carrier. Let the recipient know why you appreciate him or her. Use details. For example, if you love that your husband cleaned the car, write something like, "A fresh car, and you make me smile. I love you. XOX." Or if your mom picked up your kids from dance class, try something like, "Ballet is beautiful and so are you. I love you. Thanks for always helping out." Then mail the letter. Putting it in an envelope, sealing it, and stamping it give a little extra love-letter pizzazz to your note.

Move, Move, Move!

If you want to live with passion and energy, being active is key. Exercise is important, of course, but so is living actively between workouts. Movement energizes you and ignites passion in all parts of your life. Here are simple things you can do anytime, even if you are not in your gym clothes or any-where near a gym:

- Breathe deeply.
- Hold your tummy tight.
- Stretch your arms out wide.
- Do some side bends.

- Lunge up the staircase.
- Do calf raises while waiting in line.
- Don't drive through: actually park and walk.
- Offer to help carry something (a neighbor's groceries, a coworker's bags, or boxes that need to be moved).
- Twist and punch to whittle the waist and move those arms.
- Follow the next-level rule: push your activity up a notch by standing instead of sitting, walking instead of standing, running instead of walking.

Experience Life by Adding Sparkle to Your Soul

My mother always taught me that a little lip gloss goes a long way. She always said that taking just a minute extra for some self-care can really make a difference in the way you feel. And although she was a licensed cosmetologist, Mom also taught me that real beauty cannot come from expensive makeup, a new hairstyle, or designer clothing. It comes from within.

I do like makeup—it's fun to play with and can change your look and sometimes your mood. I'm always amazed at how a swipe of lip gloss can add sparkle to your face. But I've also learned that there are many ways to add sparkle to your soul too. Smiling at a stranger, lending a helping hand, noticing the color of the leaves, dancing with your kids—these are things that make your soul smile, sparkle, shine.

We all have a light inside of us. Sometimes it's shining strong; other times we need to reignite our spark for life. Here are some soul sparklers for you—along with one last assignment for you at the very end of the list:

To Sparkle Every Day

- Smile. Be compassionate in all human interactions.

- Show public appreciation. Praise someone in front of family or coworkers, on a blog, or in some other public way.

- Write a joy list of your ten favorite things.

To Sparkle in Your Community

- Volunteer at your local shelter, soup kitchen, or senior center. Get to know the people inside and connect with them by listening and sharing stories.

- Clean up the park, the streets, or any place that needs some TLC. Dive in and beautify your community.

- Be a good neighbor by watering lawns, helping to remove snow, or stopping by with a pot of hot homemade soup on a cold winter day.

- Connect with children. Be a coach or umpire, color with a neighbor's toddler, offer to babysit, hold a newborn baby, or visit a children's hospital. Nothing makes the soul sparkle like experiencing the world through the eyes of a child.

- Vote in local elections, go to town meetings, and contribute your special gifts and unique talents to enrich your community.

- Share your stuff—the lawn mower, a bike, your car—there are always times when a neighbor could use some help but may feel awkward asking.

- Create community events: potluck suppers, picnics, horse and buggy rides, caroling, or open-house mixers with tea and cookies.

- Spread good news about neighbors' new grandchildren, promotions, and business ventures.
- Connect in your online community as well. Contribute or comment to blogs you read, or reach out to an old friend on Facebook with a happy memory or a random note.

To Add Sparkle to Your Physical Self

- What you eat affects everything you do, think, see, and feel. It affects your productivity, attitude, relationships, and mood. Eat real food and feel real good; eat junk and feel like junk.

- Take two minutes in the morning and two minutes in the evening just to breathe.

- Get down! Doing yoga poses such as a downward dog, upward-facing dog, or hero pose for a couple of minutes a day is a great way to stretch your muscles, improve flexibility, and clear your mind.

• Get some sleep. Help yourself sleep better by not eating anything at least three hours before bedtime and preparing your body to relax. If your mind won't let you rest and keeps spinning with whatever has given you the blues, instead of counting sheep, count your blessings.

• Warm your sheets before bed. Soft sheets, just out of the dryer make for a cozy night and happier mornings.

• Move, move, move, and move some more!

• Get a massage. If your budget is tight, check out massage therapy schools that offer extremely discounted rates (or even free massages).

• Practice gratitude regularly. Give thanks even during difficult times. Gratitude relieves stress and tension in the body and makes your soul sparkle.

To Sparkle at Home

• Circles suggest harmony and unity, so make sure you have circles, such as wreaths, on your front door and inside your home.

• Once you've read a book, write a note in the cover about your thoughts on it, your favorite part, something personal. Create a book-giveaway basket, and every time someone enters your home, invite them to pick a book at random without looking inside. Whatever they choose will be the message they are meant to receive.

• Rid energy drainers: fill holes, fix squeaks, and replace bulbs and batteries for a clean, updated look.

To Sparkle at Work

• Write a morning to-do list. Bonus points for smiling when writing it.

• Organize your space bit by bit. Start by organizing just the space you're working in right now.

Chapter Eight - E is for Engage and Experience

- Unsubscribe from every junk mail e-mail list you are on.

- Contribute toward creating a positive, pleasant work environment. Do not participate in gossip sessions with coworkers, as they just create negativity all around.

- Take a dance break—yes, at work.

- Give someone a list of all they've done that you're grateful for. Take a few minutes to make a list of ten or twenty things a coworker or colleague has done that you appreciate.

To Sparkle Behind the Wheel

- Tune your radio to something that makes you smile, laugh, or just relax—upbeat or soothing music, a book on tape, or your favorite talk radio show.

- Use your drive time to reconnect and fully experience the present moment.

- Send prayers and peaceful thoughts to crazy drivers. Don't get caught up in their road rage.

- Post your favorite quote or affirmation somewhere in your car.

- Silence your phone, especially on short trips. Not only will this create a more peaceful drive, but you won't be tempted to check it every time it dings or buzzes. Nothing is so urgent that it's worth risking your life or the lives of others on the road. Or create special ring tones for expected/emergency calls.

- Take a random drive to the beach, the mountains, or a park and watch the sun set or rise.

To Sparkle While Shopping

- Let someone with just one item skip ahead of you and your cart full of groceries at the checkout line.

- Ask the mother with her hands full if she needs help opening the car door.

- Put your shopping cart back where it belongs.

- If you see an item in the wrong section, return it to its proper place.

- Buy the person in line behind you at the drive-through a cup of coffee.

- Purchase something to donate—extra canned goods, toys, hats, or mittens. Or make something by hand and give it away.

Eat Sparkle-Worthy Breakfasts

- Cooked oat cereal with cinnamon
- High-fiber cereal with almond milk and fruit
- Egg-white omelet with salsa and low-fat cheese in a tortilla
- Egg-white omelet with chipotle and fresh basil
- Toasted whole-wheat bread with a teaspoon of apple butter
- Toasted wheat english muffin with avocado and tomato
- Protein drink with fruit and wheat germ in a smoothie
- Plain low-fat yogurt with coconut extract and berries
- Pumpkin bran muffin with ½ teaspoon almond butter

Eat Sparkle-Worthy Lunches

- Chicken salad made with apples, celery, tarragon, lemon, and fennel tossed in a Dijon-yogurt dressing
- Tuna salad made with Dijon mustard and ½ teaspoon mayo on Wasa crackers
- Soup made with low-sodium broth, lots of veggies, and delicious herbs and seasonings

- Green leafy salad topped with chicken, goat cheese, apples, pears, pecans and tossed with olive oil and a splash of champagne vinegar

- Spinach leaves used as wraps for turkey, tomato, and hummus

- Fresh mozzarella, sun-dried tomato, and basil in a whole-grain pita

- Smoked salmon and cream cheese on leaf lettuce with crostini and tapenade

- Chili made with turkey or vegetarian, with beans, corn, celery, tomato, and onions

Chapter Eight - E is for Engage and Experience

Eat Sparkle-Worthy Dinners

- Whole-grain pizza with fresh mozzarella, tomato, and basil
- Mediterranean chicken with tomato, olives, and white beans
- Broiled tilapia with rosemary and lemon served with couscous
- Chicken with lemon, olive oil, capers, and Dijon mustard
- Wild salmon with fresh ginger and spices served over rosemary asparagus
- Vegetable stir-fry with olive oil and low-sodium soy sauce
- Grilled peanut shrimp made with natural peanut butter, fresh lime juice, cayenne pepper, and almond milk
- Chicken kebabs served with brown rice and grilled pears
- Seafood crock-pot paella made with tomatoes, scallops, tilapia, and veggies served over brown rice

Take Action
What Makes You Sparkle?

Here's your final activity: write down five things that make your soul sparkle and share them with your online community. Have fun with it!

Acknowledgments

A huge thank you to my husband, my rock, my best friend, and our two precious gifts and my greatest teachers, Millana Elle (LuLu) and Ewing James (Little Man) — like everything good in our lives, this was a family effort. I couldn't have done this without you guys - we did it together, and I am so grateful. I also want to thank LuLu for the beautiful drawing of the tight rope walker on the back cover of this book - I am so proud of you, my inspirista!! Little Man, my 'son shine', thank you for your ideas, and amazing memory - so much of your input helped with the writing of this book!!

To my parents—words can't express the gratitude in my heart for all you do for our family, for always lifting me up, and standing beside me no matter what. Every girl should be so lucky. 143

Grandma Millie, I know you are up there helping and believing, too. And Miss Mary Lou, too. I think of you both every day, and some pearl of wisdom you shared with me pops into my heart always. You are angels - I love and miss you both so very much.

To my mother-in-law, Ellie, you are another earth angel to us in so many ways!! Thank you for raising your son to be such a good, loving husband and father.

To Michael's Grandma Mary, I hear so many beautiful stories about you. Michael remembers sitting on the oatmeal can by your bedside, and you always making him feel loved. We thank you for all you did to help out, and just be there for Michael's family.

To all my family members, friends, and extended family - your love and support and guidance is a gift. Thank you for always being there for me, and encouraging me no matter what.

To my early morning crew at QuickChek, I have to thank you for always having my Chocolate Macadamia Nut Coffee ready to go at o'dark thirty!! It makes my day and so does seeing each of you!

To the women who have taken my courses, and our brown bag lunchers at The Domesticated Dad, thank you for opening your hearts to learning from each other and exploring life together.

I am grateful to God for all the mercy and grace He's given to me. I know that if just one person reads this book and it reminds them of their awesomeness and that they are a magnificently made child of God, then the words have done their work.

About the Author

Jennifer Tuma-Young is the founder of Inspirista Lifestyle Design and creator of the Inspired Girl Blog. Over the past fifteen years, she has worked with thousands of women, and traveled the country speaking at events, for nonprofits, and in the media. Now, in her daily life, she is a proud momma of her two most precious gifts from God, and she is the co-creative force behind her family business, The Domesticated Dad Catering Company where she works with her incredible food-creating husband serving awesome, homemade meals in their community.

To connect with her online, sign up for the mailing list, download resources, and read the blog, visit http://inspiredgirl.net

Made in the USA
Middletown, DE
06 December 2017